Power Maths
Year 2
Practice Book 2A

White Rose Maths

White Rose Maths Edition

What do you look like?
Draw a picture of you.

T0386073

This book belongs to _____ .

My class is _____ .

Series editor: Tony Staneff

Lead author: Josh Lury

Consultant (first edition): Professor Liu Jian

Author team (first edition): Tony Staneff, Josh Lury, Kelsey Brown, Liu Jian, Zhang Dan and Wang Mingming

Pearson

Contents

We will practise different ways to solve problems!

2

Let's go and do some maths!

How to use this book

Let's see how this Practice Book works!

Use the Textbook first to learn how to solve this type of problem.

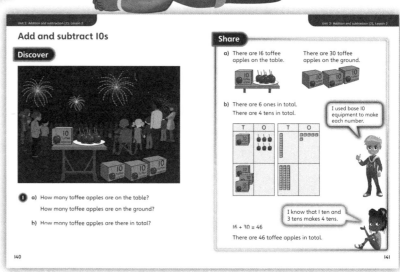

This shows you which Textbook page to use.

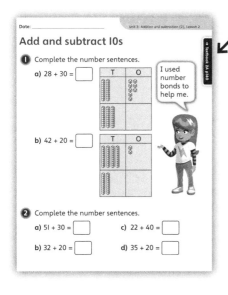

Have a go at questions by yourself using this Practice Book. Use what you have learnt.

Challenge questions make you think hard!

Questions with this light bulb make you think differently.

Reflect

Each lesson ends with a Reflect question so you can show how much you have learnt.

Show what you have done in My Power Points at the back of this book.

Reflect

Fill in the missing digits to complete the number sentences.

☐6 – ☐0 = 76   ☐6 – ☐0 = 36

Did you get the same as your partner?

105

My journal

At the end of a unit your teacher will ask you to fill in My journal.

This will help you show how much you can do now that you have finished the unit.

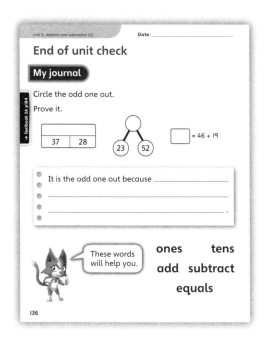

Unit 3: Addition and subtraction (2)   Date: _____

End of unit check

My journal

→ Textbook 2A p184

Circle the odd one out.

Prove it.

| 37 | 28 |

23   52   ☐ = 46 + 19

It is the odd one out because _____
_____
_____.

These words will help you.

ones   tens

add   subtract

equals

136

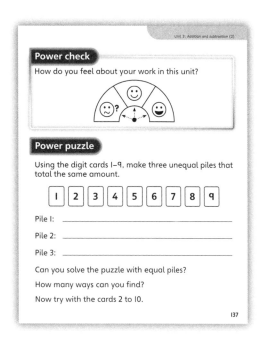

Unit 3: Addition and subtraction (2)

Power check

How do you feel about your work in this unit?

Power puzzle

Using the digit cards 1–9, make three unequal piles that total the same amount.

| 1 | 2 | 3 | 4 | 5 | 6 | 7 | 8 | 9 |

Pile 1: _____

Pile 2: _____

Pile 3: _____

Can you solve the puzzle with equal piles?

How many ways can you find?

Now try with the cards 2 to 10.

137

Date: _____

Numbers to 20

1 Fill in the missing numbers.

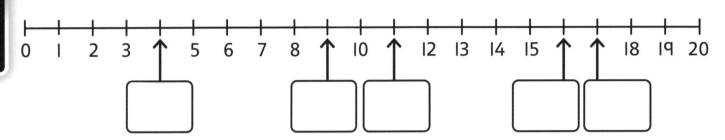

2 Cross out numbers **less than** 13.

Circle numbers **greater than** 17.

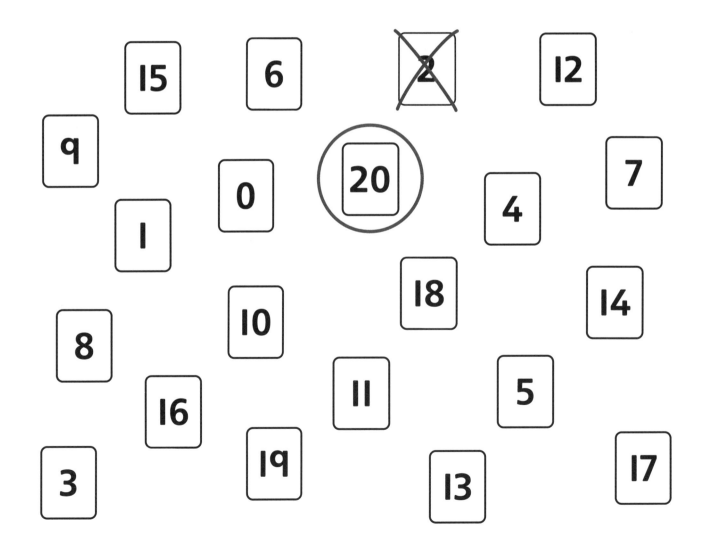

3 Write the numbers.

a) 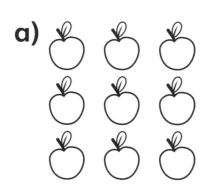

c)

b)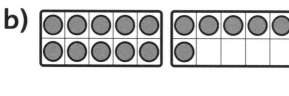

d)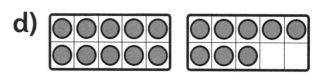

4 Complete the part-whole models.

a)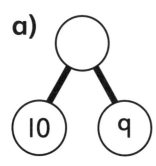

c)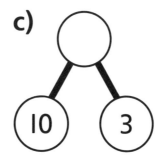

e)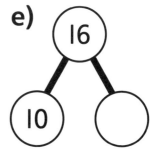

b)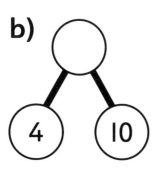

d)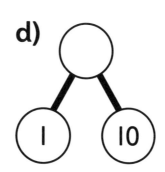

f)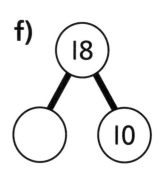

5 Write each set of numbers in order.

CHALLENGE

a)

| 11 | 3 | 10 |

Smallest ☐ ☐ ☐ Greatest

b)

| 16 | 6 | 20 |

Smallest ☐ ☐ ☐ Greatest

c)

| 14 | 19 | 9 | 6 |

Smallest ☐ ☐ ☐ ☐ Greatest

Reflect

Which numbers are between 8 and 15?

_____

_____

_____

Date: _____

Count in 10s

→ Textbook 2A p12

1 Complete the counts.

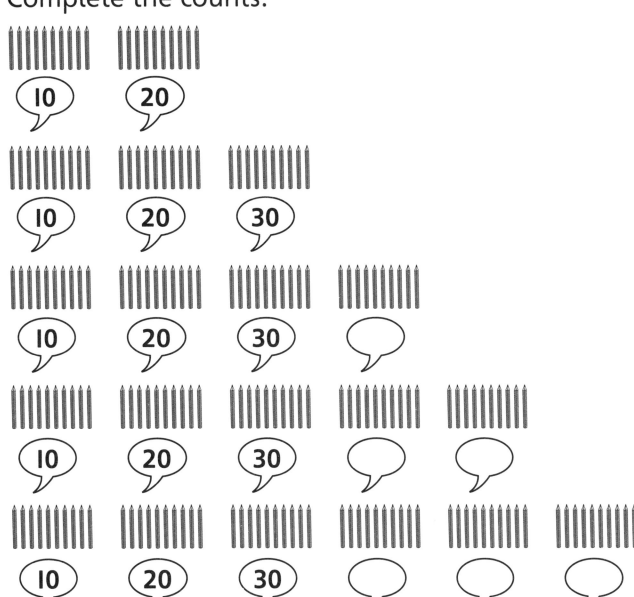

2 Complete the number track.

0	10	20	30						90

3 Shade all the 10s.

1	2	3	4	5	6	7	8	9	10
11	12	13	14	15	16	17	18	19	20
21	22	23	24	25	26	27	28	29	30
31	32	33	34	35	36	37	38	39	40
41	42	43	44	45	46	47	48	49	50
51	52	53	54	55	56	57	58	59	60
61	62	63	64	65	66	67	68	69	70
71	72	73	74	75	76	77	78	79	80
81	82	83	84	85	86	87	88	89	90
91	92	93	94	95	96	97	98	99	100

4 Write each number.

a)

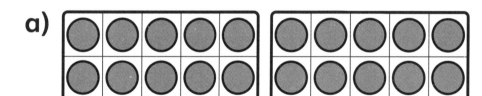

b)

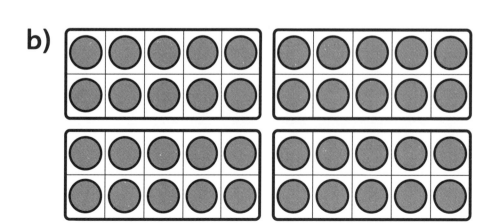

5 **a)** Circle 10s to make 60.

CHALLENGE

b) Circle 10s to make 70.

Reflect

Count in 10s to 100.

Count with a partner. Take it in turns.

Date: _____

Count in 10s and 1s

→ Textbook 2A p16

1 Count the cans.

☐ cans

2 Count the cubes.

☐ cubes

3 Count the dots.

☐ dots

4 Is Kat correct?

Show a partner using counters and ten frames.

2 tens are the same as 20 ones.

Kat

5 Count by making 10s.

a)

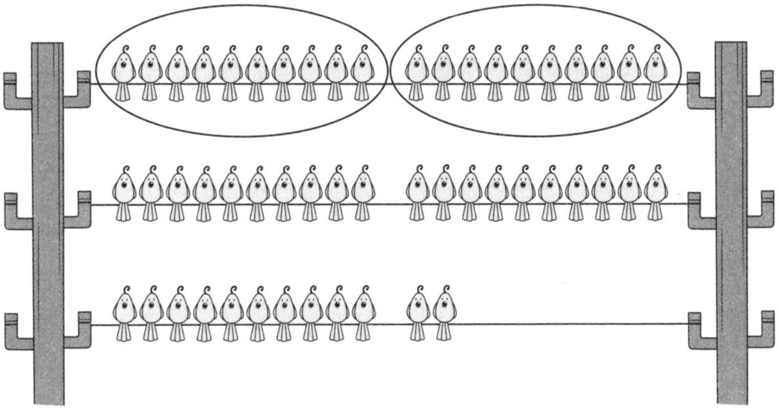

[ ] birds

b)

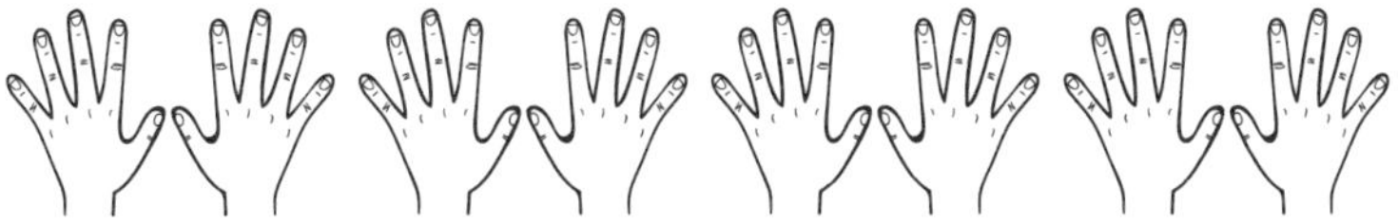

[ ] fingers

c)

[ ] cakes

6 Count in 10s and 1s.

a)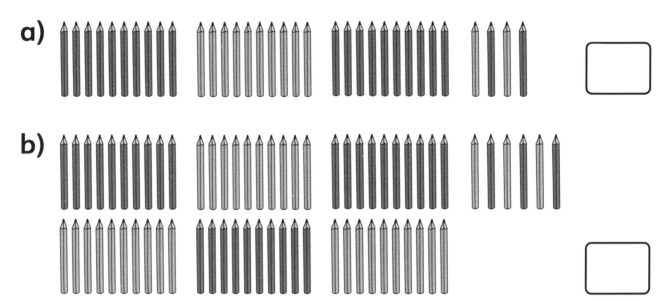

b)

7 Play a game.

Count out 99 counters.

Arrange them to show 10s and 1s.

Try to make different patterns.

CHALLENGE

Reflect

Count these with a partner.

Date: _____

Recognise 10s and 1s

→ Textbook 2A p20

1 Count in 10s and 1s.

a)

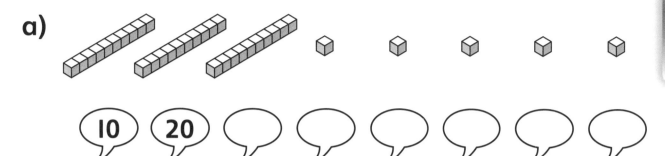

b)

2 Write the numbers.

a)

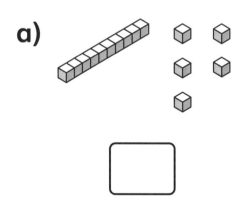

b)

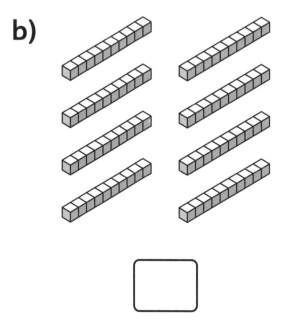

3 Draw lines to join the matching numbers.

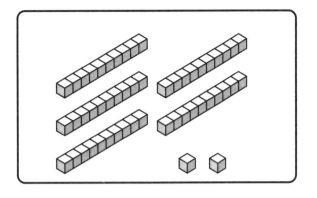

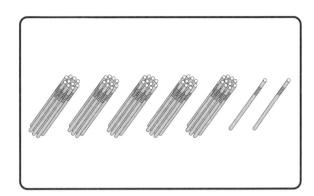

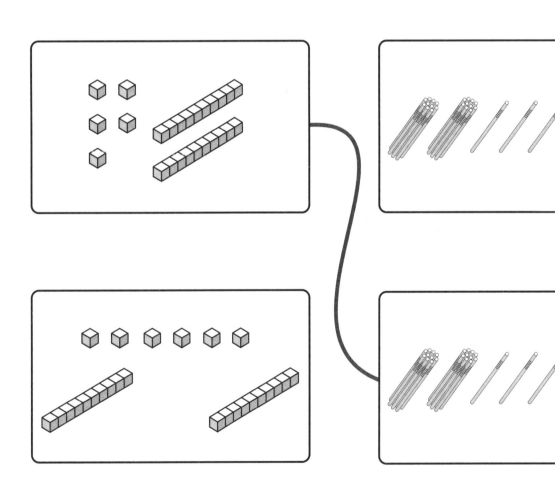

4 Write these numbers.

a)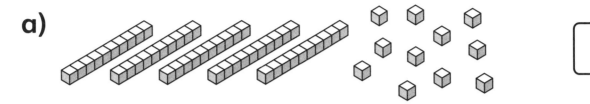

b)

---

5 Emma says you need 70 cubes to make this tower.

Prove Emma is wrong by counting in 10s.

Emma is wrong. You need ☐ cubes to make the tower.

CHALLENGE

Reflect

Make a picture from base 10 rods and cubes.

Count the total.

Here is an example.

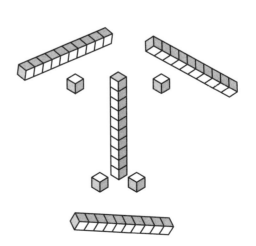

Date: _____

Build a number from 10s and 1s

→ Textbook 2A p24

1 Use base 10 equipment to make each number.

a) Draw 30.

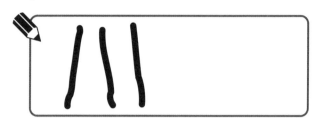

c) Draw 50.

b) Draw 40.

d) Draw 70.

2 **a)** Draw 20.

d) Draw 40.

b) Draw 22.

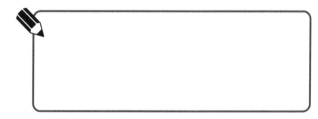

e) Draw 42.

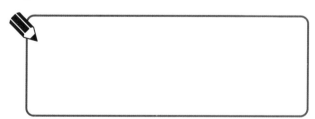

c) Draw 29.

f) Draw 49.

3 Draw lines to show matching sets of 3.
One has been done for you.

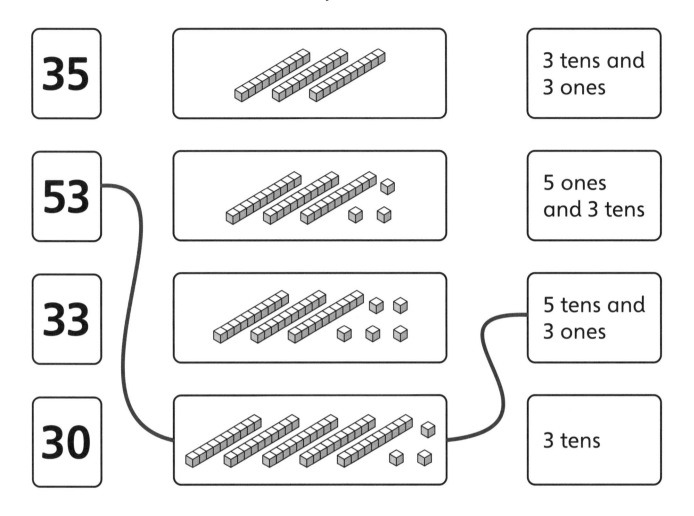

4 Draw pictures and complete the sentences.

a) ✎

45 is ☐ tens and ☐ ones.

b) ✎

☐ is 6 tens and 2 ones.

5 **a)** Draw and write two different numbers that have 4 tens and some ones.

CHALLENGE

b) Draw and write two different numbers which have 4 ones and some tens.

Reflect

Make or draw each number.

Tell a partner what is the same and what is different.

| 31 | 13 | 30 |

Date: _____

Use a place value grid

1 Write each number.

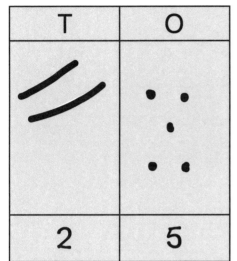

T	O
2	5

T	O

T	O

2 Draw tens and ones.

T	O
1	7

T	O
3	7

T	O
5	7

3 Write the numbers.

a)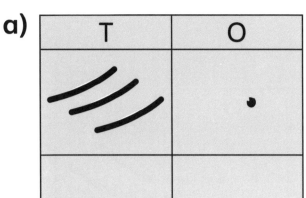

b)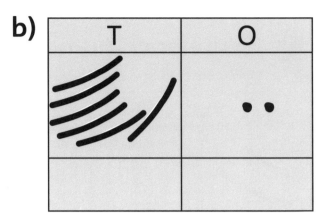

4 Write the numbers.

a)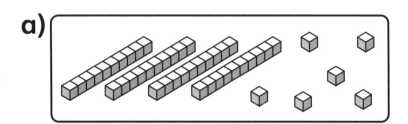

T	O

b)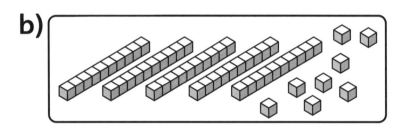

T	O

c)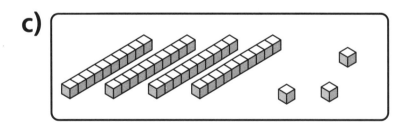

T	O

d)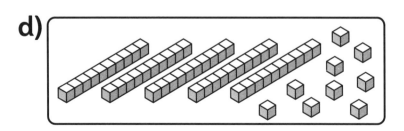

T	O

5 Make 6 different numbers from these cards.

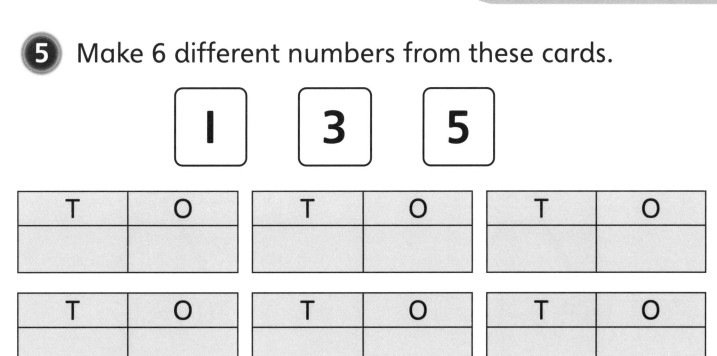

T	O

T	O

T	O

T	O

T	O

T	O

6 Mia thinks of a 2-digit number.

She says: 'The 10s digit is **1 more** than the 1s digit. One of my digits is a 5.'

What numbers could Mia be thinking of? Discuss with a partner.

Reflect

What does the 8 stand for in each number? Explain your answers to a partner.

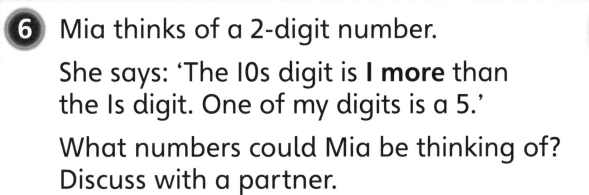

| 85 | 80 | 8 | 82 |

Date: _____

Partition numbers to 100

1 Complete the part-whole models.

a)

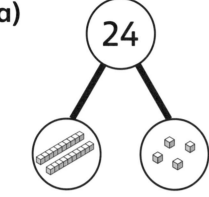

24

24

20

b)

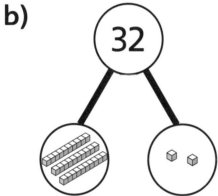

32

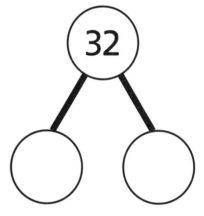

32

2 Max has made a number from straws.

Complete his part-whole model.

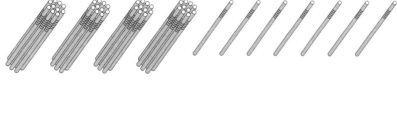

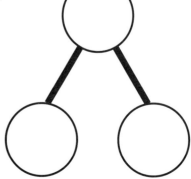

3 Complete the part-whole models.

a)

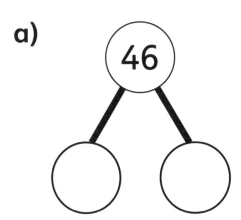

b)

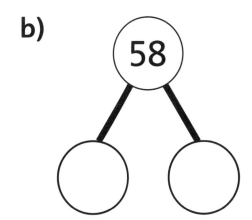

4 Complete the part-whole models.

a)

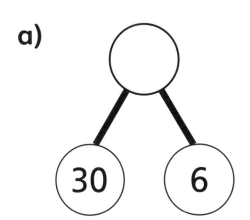

c)

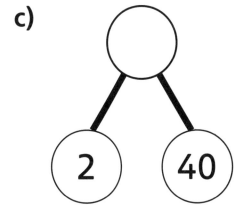

b)

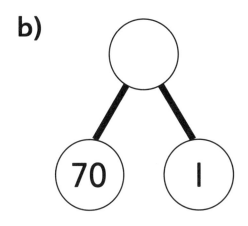

d)

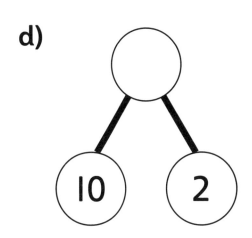

5 Complete the part-whole models.

a)

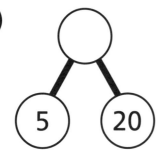

b)

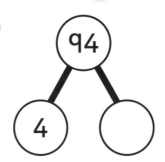

6 Which part-whole models are correct?
Put a tick or a cross.
Explain the mistakes to a partner.

CHALLENGE

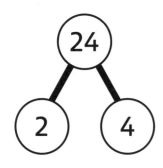 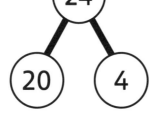 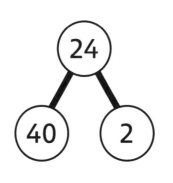 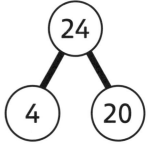

Reflect

Draw and complete your own part-whole model.

Ask a partner to check if it is correct.

Date: _____

Partition numbers flexibly within 100

1 Complete the part-whole models.

a)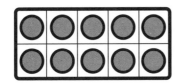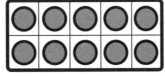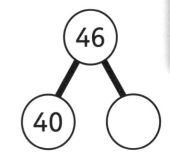

b)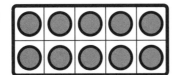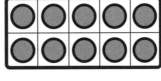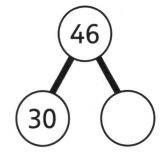

c)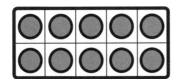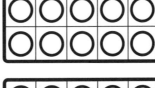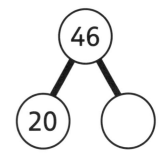

Textbook 2A p36

2 Use the partitions to complete the part-whole models.

a)

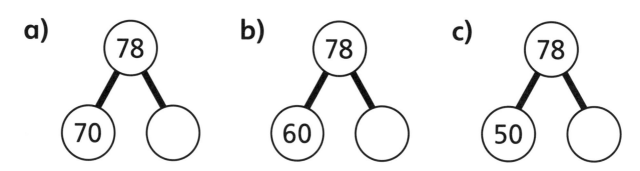

b)

c)

3 Complete the part-whole models.

a)

b)

c)

4 Complete the part-whole models.

a)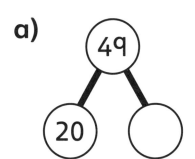

b)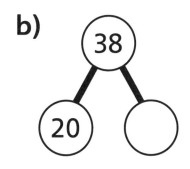

c)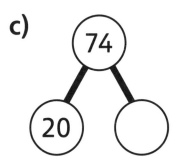

5 The whole is the same. Find the parts.

a)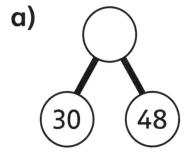

b)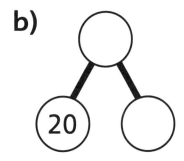

c)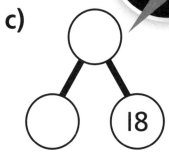

Reflect

How many ways can you find to partition 64?

Draw part-whole models.

Date: _____

Write numbers to 100 in expanded form

 Use 10s and 1s to complete the number sentences.

a)

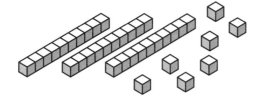

30 + 7 = ☐

b)

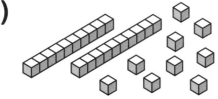

☐ + ☐ = 29

2 Draw lines to match the pairs.

40 + 6		61
30 + 5		53
60 + 1		46
50 + 3		35

3 Complete the number sentences.

a) $17 = 10 + \boxed{}$

b) $38 = 30 + \boxed{}$

c) $71 = 70 + \boxed{}$

d) $20 + 5 = \boxed{}$

e) $30 + 8 = \boxed{}$

f) $60 + 2 = \boxed{}$

4 Complete the number sentences.

a) $24 = \boxed{} + 4$

$34 = \boxed{} + 4$

$44 = \boxed{} + 4$

b) $73 = \boxed{} + 3$

$75 = \boxed{} + 5$

$79 = \boxed{} + 9$

5 Write each number in expanded form using 10s and 1s.

a) $39 = \boxed{} + \boxed{}$

b) $57 = \boxed{} + \boxed{}$

c) $\boxed{} + \boxed{} = 13$

6 Is Eddie correct?

Eddie

7 + 30 = 73

Explain your answer to a partner.

7 Complete the number sentences.

CHALLENGE

53 = 50 + ☐   53 = 30 + ☐

53 = 40 + ☐   53 = 20 + ☐

I will make the numbers
out of 10s and Is to help me.

Reflect

Show 43 in different ways.

10s on a number line to 100

→ Textbook 2A p44

1 Fill in the missing numbers.

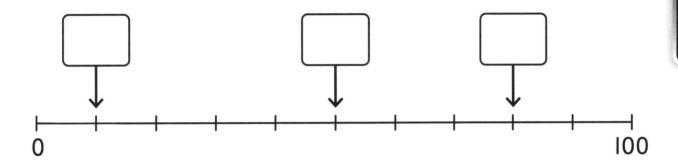

2 Join each number to the number line.

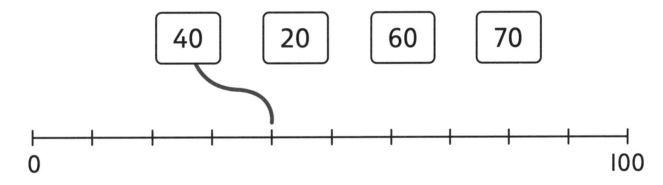

3 Complete the number line.

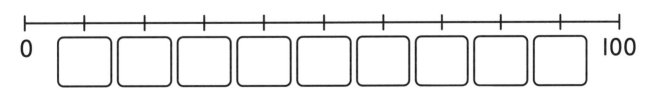

a) Join each set to the number line.

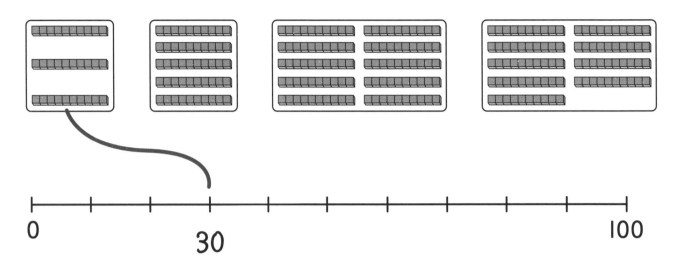

b) Draw 10s rods to match the numbers on the number line.

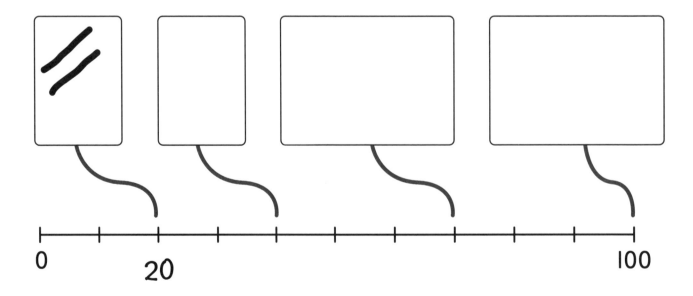

5 Write the missing numbers.

a)

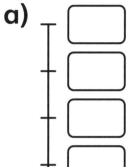

```
[   ]
[   ]
[   ]
[   ]
[   ]
[   ]
[   ]
20
10
0
```

b)

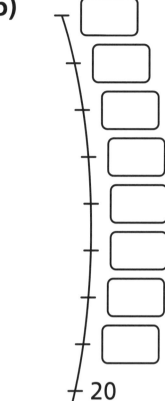

```
[   ]
[   ]
[   ]
[   ]
[   ]
[   ]
[   ]
20
10
0
```

Reflect

Draw your own 0 to 100 number line. Label the 10s.

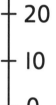

Date: _____

10s and 1s on a number line to 100

1 Write the number.

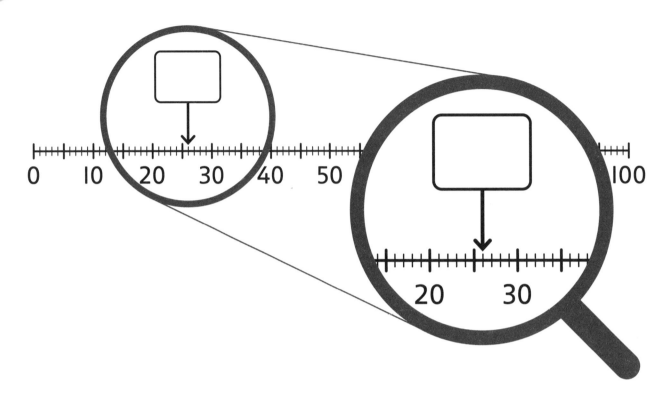

2 Write the missing numbers.

a)
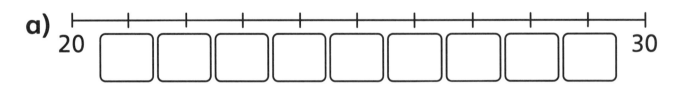

b)
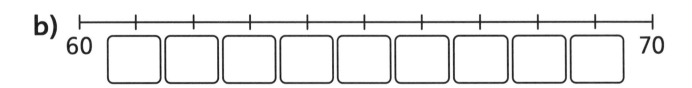

c)
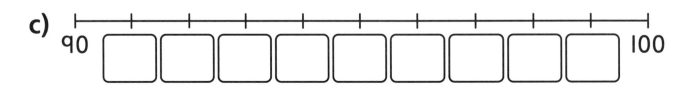

↑ Textbook 2A p48

3 Join each number to the number line.

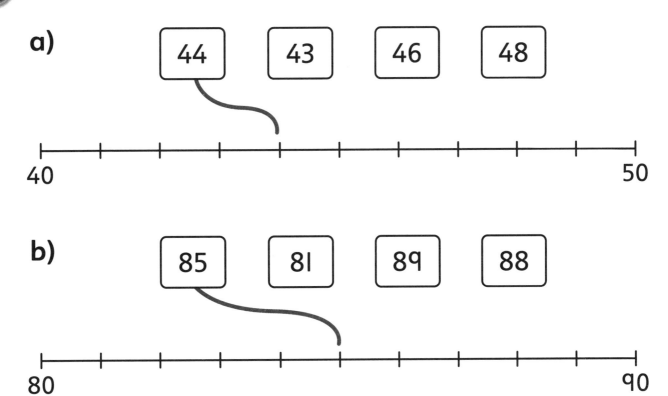

a)

44   43   46   48

40 ——————————————————————— 50

b)

85   81   89   88

80 ——————————————————————— 90

4 Write each number.

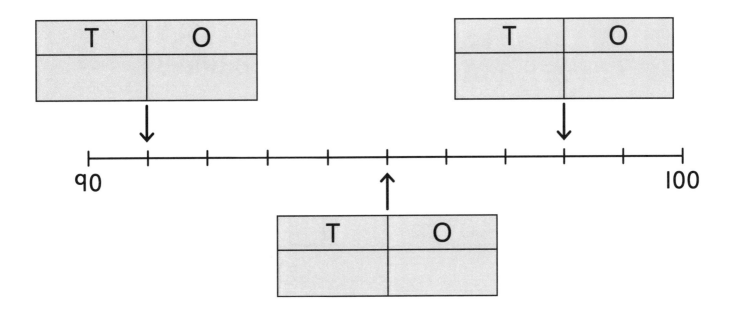

T	O

T	O

90 ——————————————————————— 100

T	O

5 Write the missing numbers.

CHALLENGE

a)

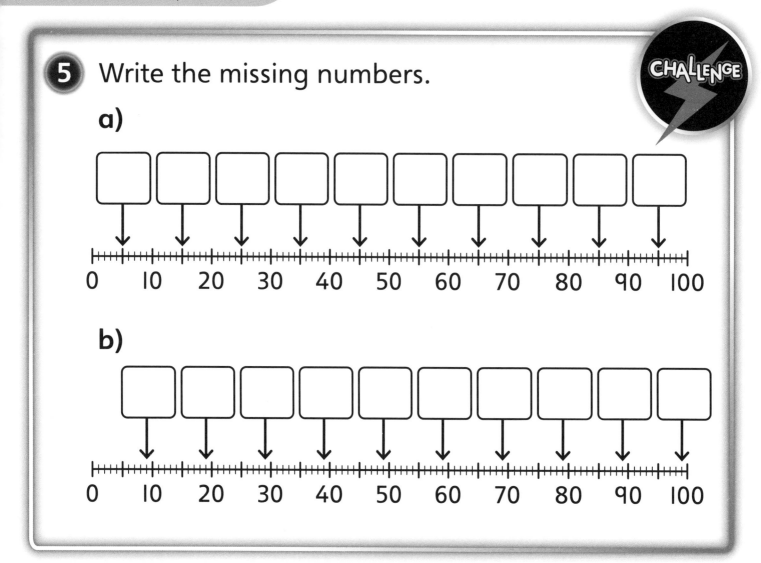

b)

Reflect

Draw a number line to show 52, 55, 58 and 59.

Estimate numbers on a number line

1 What number is each arrow pointing to?

a)

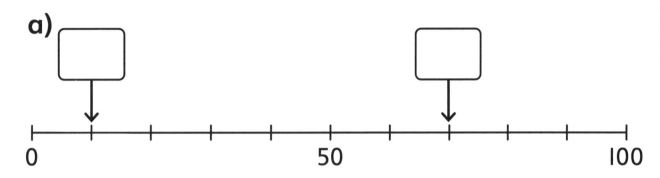

b)

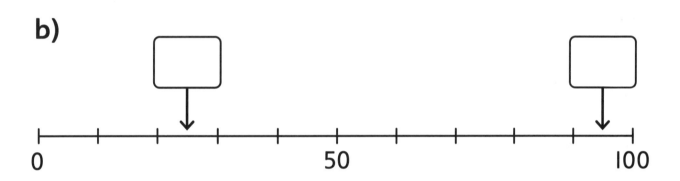

c)

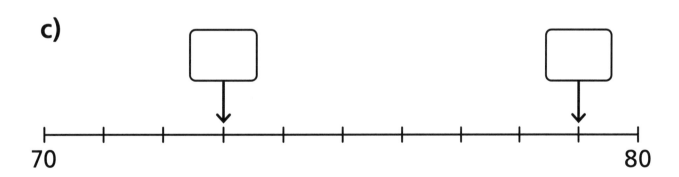

2 Fred says the arrow is pointing to the number 57.

50   60

Is Fred correct? Talk to a partner and tick the correct answer.

Yes ☐   No ☐

3 Estimate the number each arrow is pointing to.

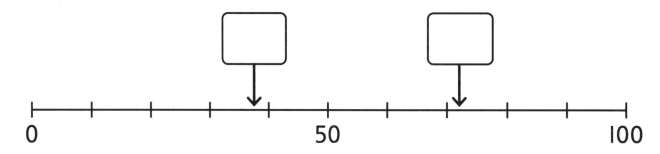

0   50   100

4 Draw an arrow from each number to its place on the number line.

| 40 | | 55 | | 89 |

0   100

5 Estimate where the number 29 is on the number line. Draw an arrow.

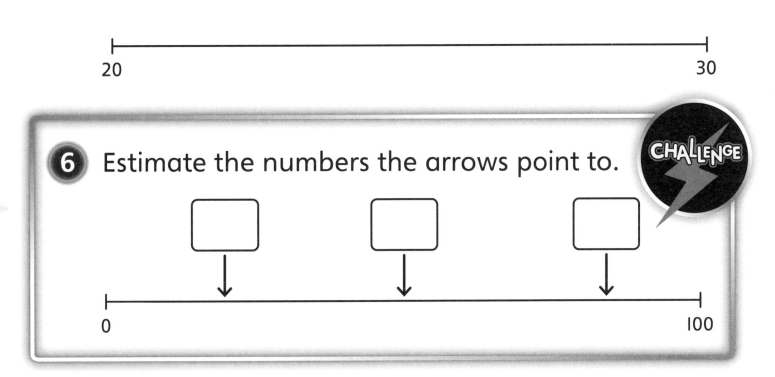

6 Estimate the numbers the arrows point to. CHALLENGE

Reflect

Estimate where each number goes. Draw arrows.

50   10   73   99

Which number was the easiest to estimate? Which was the most difficult to estimate?

Discuss with a partner.

Date: _____

Compare numbers ❶

1 **a)** Who has fewer cubes?

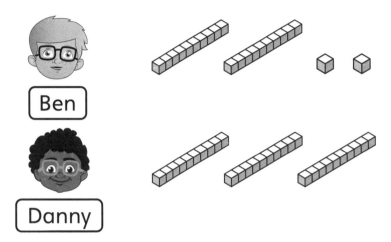

Ben

Danny

b) Who has more cubes?

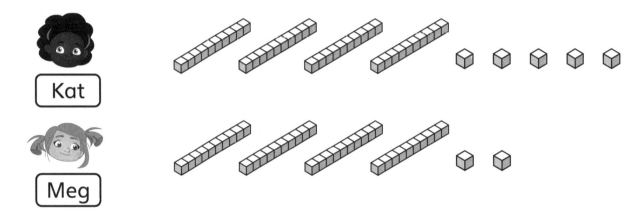

Kat

Meg

2 Complete the sentence with 'fewer' or 'more'.

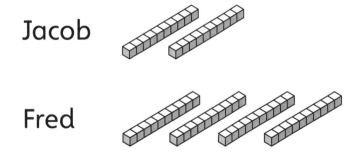

Jacob

Fred

Jacob has _____ cubes than Fred.

3 Complete the sentences.

a)

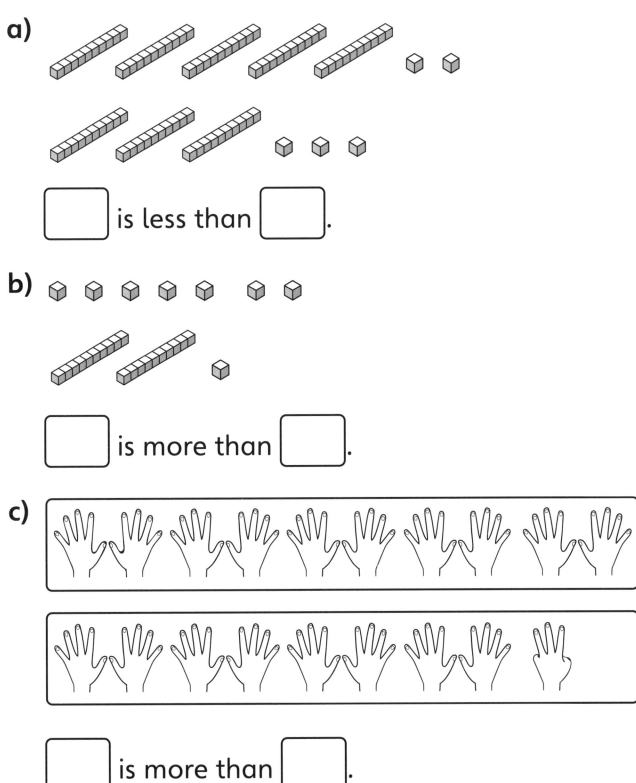

[ ] is less than [ ].

b)

[ ] is more than [ ].

c)

[ ] is more than [ ].

4 Complete the sentences with the words below.
Use the number line to help you.

| less than | | more than |

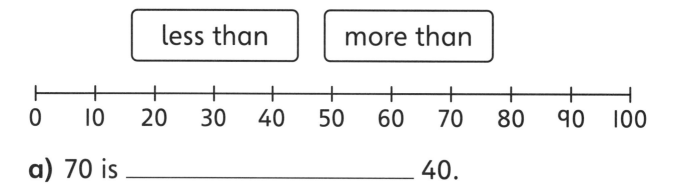

a) 70 is _____ 40.

b) 45 is _____ 60.

5 Who has the fewest cubes?

CHALLENGE

Anya ☐

Chen ☐

Reflect

Choose one of these words. Tell a partner what it means.

| fewer | | less | | more | | greater |

44

Compare numbers ❷

→ Textbook 2A p60

1 Circle the greater number in each pair.

a)

T	O
5	5

T	O
6	5

b)

T	O
5	4

T	O
4	5

c)

T	O
7	2

T	O
7	6

2 Circle the smaller number in each pair.

a)

T	O
2	1

T	O
2	9

b)

T	O
8	0

T	O
6	4

c)

T	O
4	0

T	O
	4

3 Complete the number sentences using <, > or =.

a) 40 ◯ 70

b) 32 ◯ 35

c) 48 ◯ 84

d) 19 ◯ 90

e) 50 ◯ 35

f) 26 ◯ 26

g) 70 ◯ 75

h) 75 ◯ 70

4 Choose from the words below to complete the number sentences.

less than	greater than	equal to

a) 3 tens is ＿＿＿＿＿＿＿＿＿ 30.

b) 5 tens is ＿＿＿＿＿＿＿＿＿ 4 tens and 8 ones.

c) 90 is ＿＿＿＿＿＿＿＿＿ 98.

d) 2 tens and 3 ones is ＿＿＿＿＿＿＿＿＿ 27.

5 Complete the number statements.

a) $\boxed{}9 < 50$

b) $55 < 5\boxed{}$

c) Use the same digit twice: $8\boxed{} < \boxed{}0$

6 Work out Beth's number.

CHALLENGE

Beth says:
'My number is greater than 50.
It is less than 55.
It has a 3 as one of its digits.'

Beth's number is $\boxed{}$.

I will write possible numbers in a place value grid.

Reflect

I know that 87 is more than 78 because

_____

_____

47

Date: _____

Order numbers

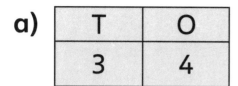

1 Tick the **smallest** number.

a)

T	O
3	4

T	O
6	2

T	O
2	1

b)

T	O
5	2

T	O
6	0

T	O
5	1

c)

14   35   47

2 Tick the **greatest** number.

a)

T	O
8	0

T	O
4	8

T	O
5	9

b)

T	O
1	2

T	O
7	7

T	O
7	4

c)

73   45   58

→ Textbook 2A p64

3 Sort each set of numbers from smallest to greatest.

a) 30 90 50   ☐ < ☐ < ☐

b) 48 68 28   ☐ < ☐ < ☐

c) 28 21 24   ☐ < ☐ < ☐

d) 58 55 9   ☐ < ☐ < ☐

4 Sort each set of numbers from greatest to smallest.

a) 30 90 50   ☐ > ☐ > ☐

b) 48 68 28   ☐ > ☐ > ☐

c) 28 21 24   ☐ > ☐ > ☐

d) 58 55 9   ☐ > ☐ > ☐

5 Write numbers to complete each statement.

a) 75 < ☐ < 85

c) ☐ < 88 < ☐

b) ☐ > 50 > ☐

d) 11 < ☐ < 15 < ☐

6 Use each card once to complete each statement.

| 0 | 5 | 3 | 5 | 2 | 4 |

☐☐ < ☐☐ < ☐☐

Reflect

Explain how to order these three numbers.

| 20 | 50 | 23 |

Do you look at the 10s or the 1s digits first?

Count in 2s, 5s and 10s

↳ Textbook 2A p68

 a) Count the cubes.

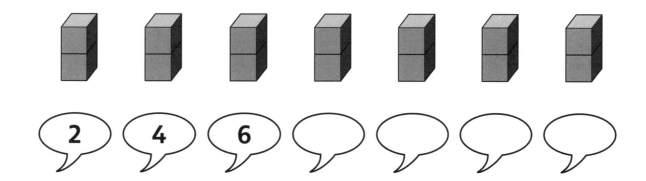

b) Count the balls.

c) Count the eggs.

2 Complete these counts.

a)

2	4	6							

b)

20	30	40					

c)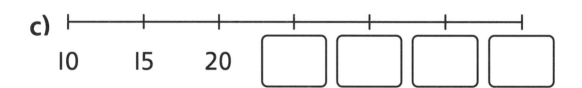

10   15   20

d) 60, 62, ☐ , ☐ , ☐ , 70

e) ☐ , ☐ , 65, 60, ☐ , ☐

3 Count the straws.

☐ straws

4 Joe says:

'I started on 20 and counted in 5s up to 50.'

Circle the numbers Joe says.

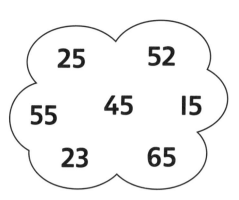

25   52

55   45   15

23   65

5 Leo says: 'I counted down in 2s from 50.'

Eva says: 'I counted up in 5s from 50.'

Which numbers will they both say?

CHALLENGE

_____

_____

_____

_____

Discuss with a partner what you notice.

Reflect

Start at 0. How far can you count in 2s in I minute?

How far can you count in 10s in I minute?

How far can you count in 5s in I minute?

Did any of your class reach 100?

Date: _____

Count in 3s

→ Textbook 2A p72

1 How many ladybirds are there?

2 How many cubes are there in each tower?

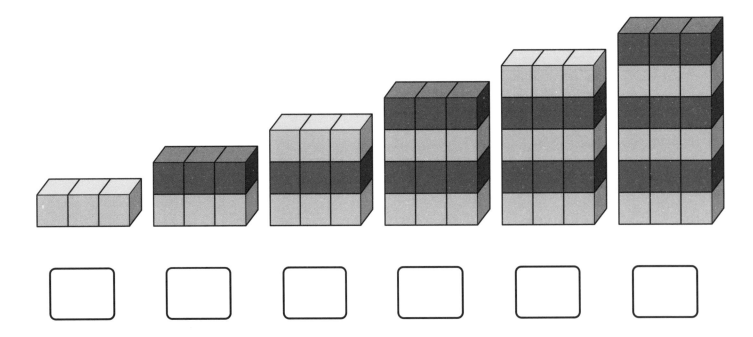

3 Write the missing numbers.

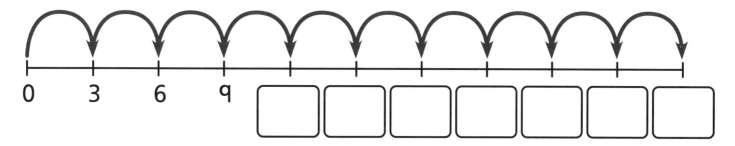

0 3 6 9 ☐ ☐ ☐ ☐ ☐ ☐ ☐

4 How many letters are there in these long words?

a) (y e s)(t e r)(d a y)

b) k i n d e r g a r t e n

5 Count up in 3s from 0. Shade in the numbers.

1	2	3	4	5	6	7	8	9	10
11	12	13	14	15	16	17	18	19	20
21	22	23	24	25	26	27	28	29	30

1	2	3	4	5	6
7	8	9	10	11	12
13	14	15	16	17	18
19	20	21	22	23	24
25	26	27	28	29	30

What do you notice about the patterns you have made?

55

6 Write the missing numbers in the boxes.

CHALLENGE

a) 3 less   3 more

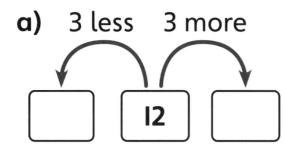

c) 3 less   3 more

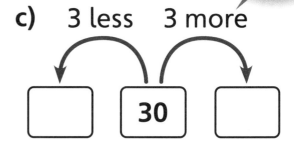

b) 3 less   3 more

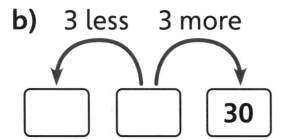

d) 3 less   3 more

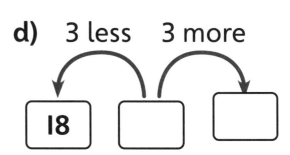

Reflect

Jodie counts in 3s from 0 to 30.

Which of the following numbers will Jodie say?

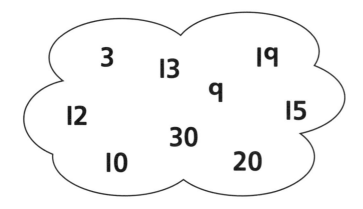

Explain to a partner how you chose your numbers.

End of unit check

→ Textbook 2A p76

My journal

Which diagram shows a different number?

Prove it.

A | 9 | | 3 |

C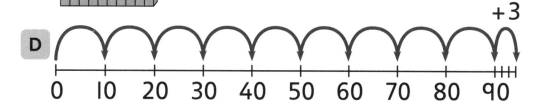

B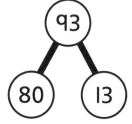

D

+3

0   10   20   30   40   50   60   70   80   90

I can prove that [   ] is a different number

because _____

_____

_____

These words will help you.

tens   ones

part-whole

number line

Power check

How do you feel about your work in this unit?

Power play

Start on 10. You can move left, right, up or down.
Choose if you want to count in 2s or 5s.
Predict which 100 you will reach.
Colour your path to 100 to test your prediction.

10	12	14	16	50	52	62	64	100
15	20	16	18	48	54	60	66	98
20	24	22	20	46	56	58	68	96
25	26	28	42	44	74	72	70	84
30	35	30	40	38	76	78	80	82
32	40	32	34	36	80	88	86	84
90	45	50	36	70	75	90	92	94
95	90	55	60	65	80	85	98	96
100	98	90	98	100	95	90	100	95

58

Date: _____

Fact families

1 Complete the fact family.

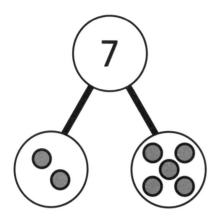

$\boxed{} + \boxed{} = \boxed{}$

$\boxed{} + \boxed{} = \boxed{}$

$\boxed{} - \boxed{} = \boxed{}$

$\boxed{} - \boxed{} = \boxed{}$

2 Complete the fact families.

a)

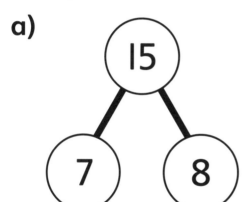

$\boxed{} + \boxed{} = \boxed{}$

$\boxed{} + \boxed{} = \boxed{}$

$\boxed{} - \boxed{} = \boxed{}$

$\boxed{} - \boxed{} = \boxed{}$

b)

13	
9	4

$\boxed{} + \boxed{} = \boxed{}$

$\boxed{} + \boxed{} = \boxed{}$

$\boxed{} - \boxed{} = \boxed{}$

$\boxed{} - \boxed{} = \boxed{}$

3 Here is a number fact.

$$7 + 3 = 10$$

Use the fact to complete the number sentences.

a) $3 + 7 = \boxed{}$

c) $10 - 7 = \boxed{}$

b) $10 - 3 = \boxed{}$

d) $10 - \boxed{} = 3$

4 **a)** Complete the part-whole model for this number fact.

$$5 + 6 = 11$$

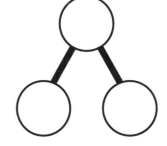

b) Write more facts to complete the fact family.

_____

_____

_____

_____

I will find 7 more facts.

5 **a)** Write the fact family for this part-whole model.

CHALLENGE

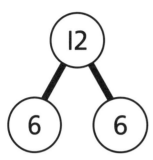

_____

_____

_____

_____

_____

_____

b) Tell a partner what you notice.

Reflect

Use the part-whole model to write as many number sentences as you can.

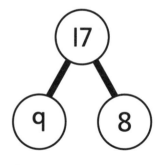

_____   _____

_____   _____

_____   _____

Date: _____

Learn number bonds

1 Solve these additions.

a) 5 + 0 = ☐

b) 4 + 0 = ☐

c) 8 + 0 = ☐

d) 0 + 1 = ☐

e) 0 + 10 = ☐

f) 0 + 2 = ☐

2 Complete these number sentences.

a) 2 + 1 = ☐

b) 7 + 1 = ☐

c) 9 + 1 = ☐

d) 1 + 5 = ☐

e) 1 + 6 = ☐

f) 5 − 1 = ☐

g) 10 − 1 = ☐

h) 2 − 1 = ☐

3 Complete these number bonds to 10.

a) 5 + ☐ = 10

b) 4 + ☐ = 10

c) 8 + ☐ = 10

d) 10 − 7 = ☐

e) 10 − 6 = ☐

f) 10 − 5 = ☐

4 Complete the number facts.

a)

$4 + 4 = \boxed{}$

c)

$3 + 3 = \boxed{}$

b)

$5 + 4 = \boxed{}$

d)

$3 + 4 = \boxed{}$

5 a) Complete the part-whole models.

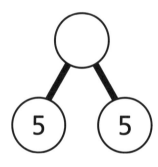 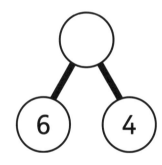 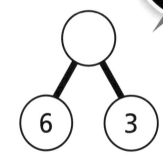

b) Complete these number sentences.

$5 + \boxed{} = 6$

$4 + \boxed{} = 6$

$3 + \boxed{} = 6$

$6 - 1 = \boxed{}$

$6 - 2 = \boxed{}$

$6 - \boxed{} = 3$

Reflect

Shade all the number bonds you know well.

+	0	1	2	3	4	5	6	7	8	9	10
0	0+0	0+1	0+2	0+3	0+4	0+5	0+6	0+7	0+8	0+9	0+10
1	1+0	1+1	1+2	1+3	1+4	1+5	1+6	1+7	1+8	1+9	
2	2+0	2+1	2+2	2+3	2+4	2+5	2+6	2+7	2+8		
3	3+0	3+1	3+2	3+3	3+4	3+5	3+6	3+7			
4	4+0	4+1	4+2	4+3	4+4	4+5	4+6				
5	5+0	5+1	5+2	5+3	5+4	5+5					
6	6+0	6+1	6+2	6+3	6+4						
7	7+0	7+1	7+2	7+3							
8	8+0	8+1	8+2								
9	9+0	9+1									
10	10+0										

Write 3 number bonds you need to practise more.

_____

_____

_____

→ Textbook 2A p88

Add and subtract two multiples of 10

1 Complete the part-whole models and number sentences.

a)

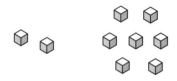

9
2   7

$2 + \boxed{} = 9$

$\boxed{} = 9 - 2$

b)

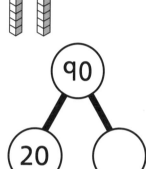

90
20

$20 + \boxed{} = 90$

$\boxed{} = 90 - 20$

2 Find the missing numbers.

a)

9	
2	7

20   70

b)

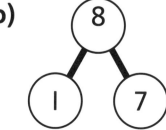

8
1   7

10	70

65

3 Use the diagrams to complete the number sentences.

a)

q	
3	6

3 + 6 = ☐

30 + 60 = ☐

9 − 3 = ☐

90 − 30 = ☐

b)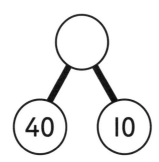

☐ = 4 + 5

50 + 40 = ☐

90 − 50 = ☐

c)

40 + 10 = ☐

50 − 40 = ☐

50 − ☐ = 40

4 **a)** Complete the part-whole models.

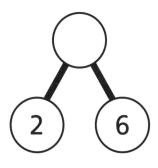 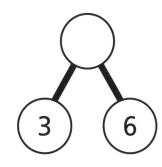 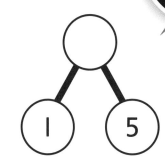

b) Complete the following.

$20 + \boxed{} = 60$ $60 - \boxed{} = 10$

$30 + \boxed{} = 60$ double $\boxed{} = 60$

$\boxed{} + 50 = 60$

CHALLENGE

Reflect

Write down some number facts related to $3 + 5 = 8$.

_____

_____

_____

Date: _____

Complements to 100 (tens)

1 What bonds to 100 are shown here?

a)

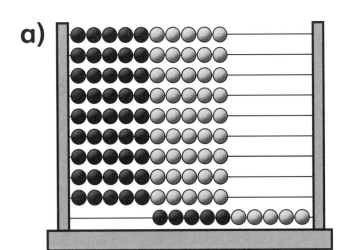

90 + ☐ = 100

c)

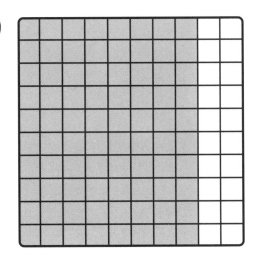

☐ + ☐ = 100

b)

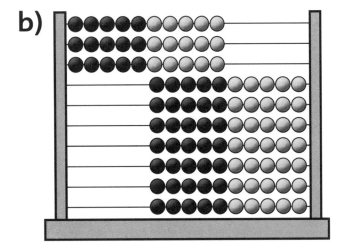

30 + ☐ = 100

d)

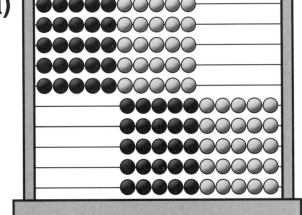

☐ + ☐ = 100

2 Complete the part-whole models.

a)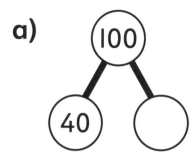

b)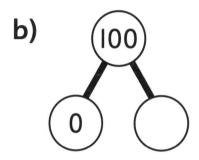

c)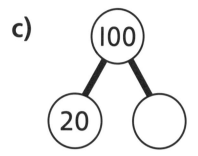

d)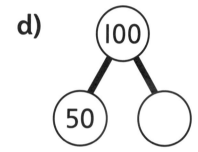

3 Which number sentences are correct?

Put a tick or a cross.

Use the part-whole model to help you.

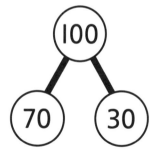

a) 30 + 100 = 70 ☐

b) 100 − 70 = 30 ☐

c) 100 − 30 = 70 ☐

d) 70 − 30 = 100 ☐

4 Draw lines to join the number bonds to 100.

| 90 | 50 | 100 | 20 | 60 | 70 |

| 50 | 40 | 80 | 0 | 30 | 10 |

5 Complete the missing number.

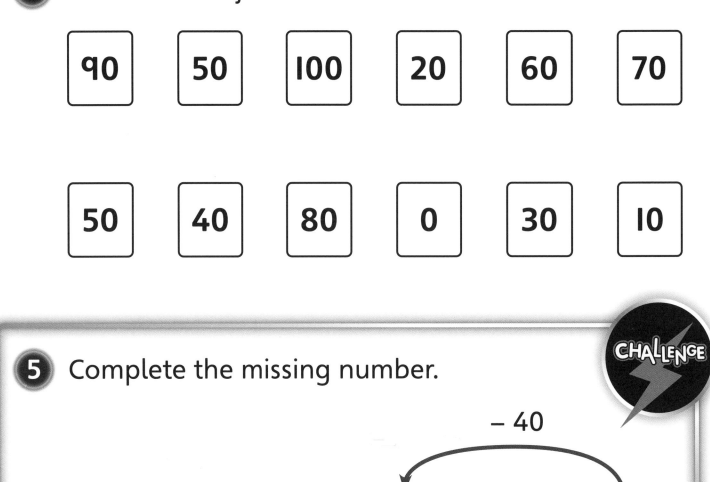

CHALLENGE

− 40

0   100

Reflect

Discuss with a partner how you can use your number bonds to 10 to work out your 10 bonds to 100.

Add and subtract 1s

1 Complete the number sentences.

a)  $23 + 4 = \boxed{}$

b)  $31 + 5 = \boxed{}$

c) $45 + 2 = \boxed{}$

2 Complete the number sentences.

a) $34 + 3 = \boxed{}$

b) $85 + 1 = \boxed{}$

c) $51 + 7 = \boxed{}$

d) $2 + 74 = \boxed{}$

3 Complete the number sentences.

a) 35 – 2 = ☐

b) 26 – 4 = ☐

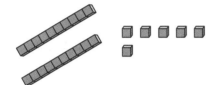

c) 48 – 7 = ☐

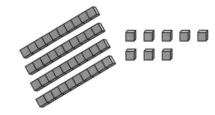

d) 37 – 2 = ☐

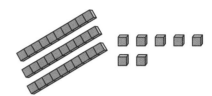

e) 19 – 6 = ☐

f) 29 – 9 = ☐

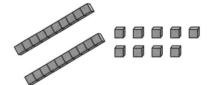

4 Join the matching pairs.

23 + 4	42 + 3
32 + 4	24 + 3
43 + 2	4 + 32

5 Solve these calculations.

a) 1 + 4 = ☐

b) 21 + 4 = ☐

c) 41 + 4 = ☐

d) 51 + 4 = ☐

e) 4 + 81 = ☐

f) 18 − 5 = ☐

g) 28 − 5 = ☐

h) 48 − 5 = ☐

i) 58 − 5 = ☐

j) 78 − 5 = ☐

6 Complete the number sentences.   CHALLENGE

17 + 1 = ☐

☐ = 41 + 6

☐ = 39 − 8

25 + ☐ = 29

45 − 5 = ☐

☐ − 5 = 32

Reflect

Discuss with a partner how to solve these calculations.

35 − 2   35 + 2

Date: _____

Add by making 10

1 Work out 8 + 5.

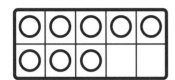 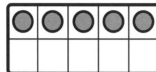

8 + ☐ + ☐ = ☐

So, 8 + 5 = ☐

2 Work out 7 + 7.

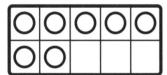 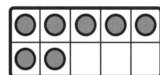

7 + ☐ + ☐ = ☐

So, 7 + 7 = ☐

3 Work out 8 + 4.

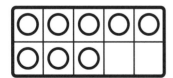 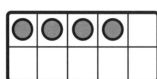

8 + ☐ + ☐ = ☐

So, 8 + 4 = ☐

First, I need to work out what makes 10.

4 Work out 8 + 6.

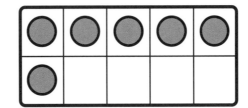

8 + ☐ + ☐ = ☐

So, 8 + 6 = ☐

5 Fred found 9 shells.

Ann found 5 shells.

How many in total?

6 Use each of these numbers once.

7   5   8   9

Make the greatest total and the smallest total.

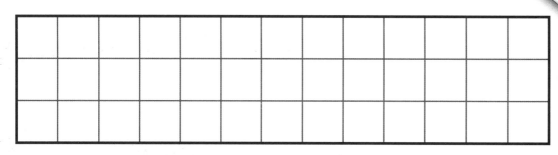

I will pick two numbers and work out the total. Then I will try a different two numbers.

Greatest: ☐ + ☐ = ☐

Smallest: ☐ + ☐ = ☐

Reflect

5 + 7 = ☐

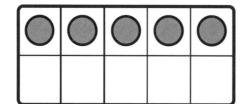

Discuss with a partner how you worked out the answer.

Add using a number line

1 Complete these additions by making 10.

Use the number lines to help you.

a) $8 + 3 =$ ☐

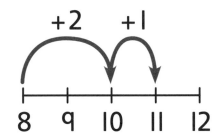

b) $8 + 6 =$ ☐

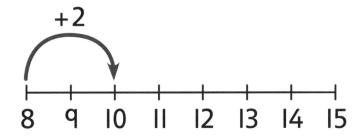

c) $7 + 5 =$ ☐

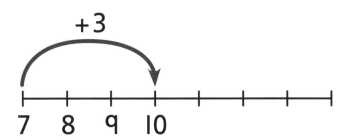

d) $9 + 4 =$ ☐

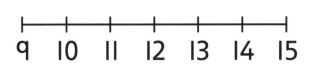

→ Textbook 2A p104

2 Complete these additions by making 10.

a) 5 + 9 = ☐

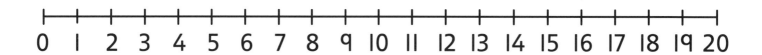

b) 3 + 9 = ☐

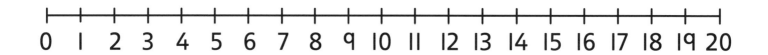

c) 9 + 9 = ☐

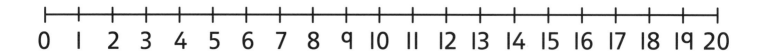

d) ☐ = 7 + 6

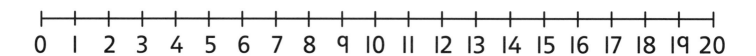

3 Circle the calculation that Hiro did.

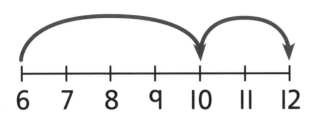

6 + 10   6 + 12

4 + 10   6 + 6

4 Kay is adding two numbers together.

What addition is she doing?

+3   +1

7

☐ + ☐ = 11

Reflect

Show how you would find 5 + 9.

Date: _____

Add three 1-digit numbers

1 Work out:

a) 2 + 4 + 2 = ☐

c) 9 + 2 + 2 = ☐

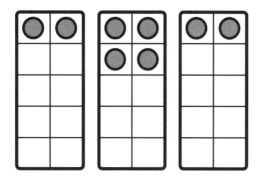

b) 1 + 6 + 3 = ☐

d) 8 + 2 + 3 = ☐

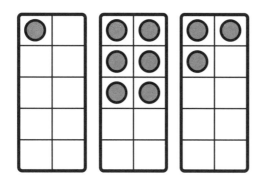
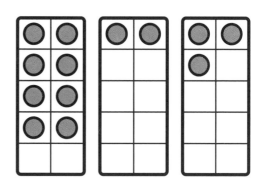

2 How many flowers are there?

7 + 6 + 4 = ☐

There are ☐ flowers.

3 Complete the part-whole models.

a)

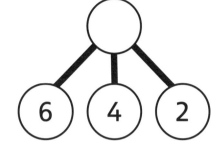

c)

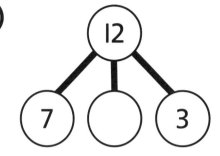

b)

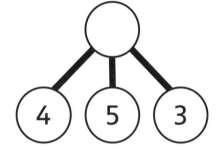

d)

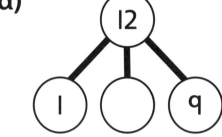

4 Complete the part-whole models in different ways, using single digits.

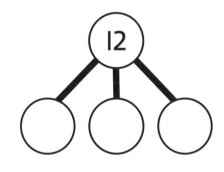

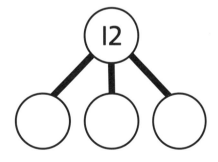

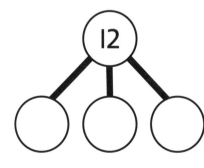

5 Work out the missing digits.

a) $2 + 8 + \boxed{} = 14$

b) $14 = 6 + 2 + \boxed{}$

c) $14 = \boxed{} + 3 + 3$

I think I will add 2 + 8 together first.

CHALLENGE

Reflect

Choose three cards to add.

What different totals can you make?

| 3 | 5 | 7 | 9 |

Compare your totals with a partner.

Who made the biggest number?

Add to the next 10

1 Complete the number sentences to make the next 10.

a)

$9 + \boxed{} = 10$

b)

$19 + \boxed{} = 20$

c)

$29 + \boxed{} = 30$

2 Complete the number sentences to make the next 10.

a)

$6 + \boxed{} = 10$

$26 + \boxed{} = 30$

b)

$8 + \boxed{} = 10$

$58 + \boxed{} = 60$

3 Complete the number sentences to make the next 10.

a)

$17 + \boxed{} = \boxed{}$

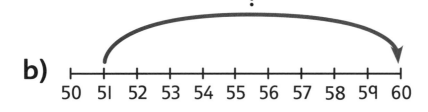

b)

$51 + \boxed{} = \boxed{}$

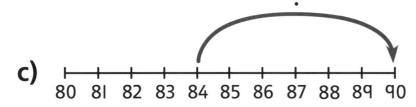

c)

$84 + \boxed{} = \boxed{}$

4 Complete the number sentences.

a) $27 + \boxed{} = 30$

b) $23 + \boxed{} = 30$

c) $31 + \boxed{} = 40$

d) $39 + \boxed{} = 40$

5 Complete the number sentences.

a) $\boxed{} + 2 = 20$

b) $\boxed{} + 2 = 40$

c) $\boxed{} + 2 = 60$

d) $\boxed{} + 5 = 10$

e) $\boxed{} + 5 = 30$

f) $\boxed{} + 5 = 50$

6 **a)** Complete these part-whole models.

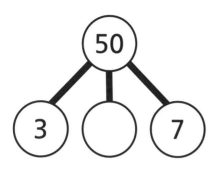

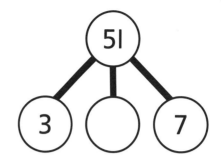

b) Complete these bar models.

90		
6		4

91		
6		4

Reflect

Complete this calculation in as many ways as you can.

$$\boxed{} + \boxed{} = 50$$

Date: _____

Add across a 10

1 How many stars are there in total?

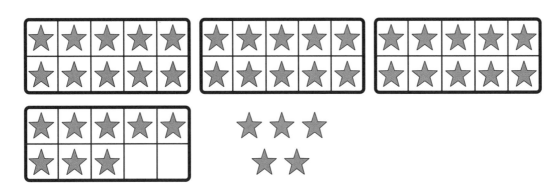

$38 + 5 = 38 + \boxed{} + \boxed{} = \boxed{}$

2 **a)** Work out 18 + 6.

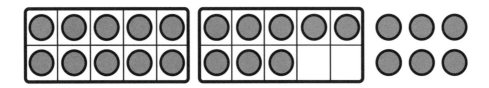

$18 + 6 = 18 + \boxed{} + \boxed{} = \boxed{}$

b) Work out 16 + 6.

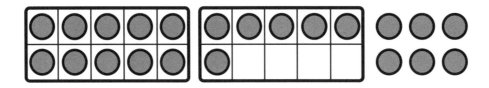

$16 + 6 = 16 + \boxed{} + \boxed{} = \boxed{}$

3 The ten frames show 26 + 7.

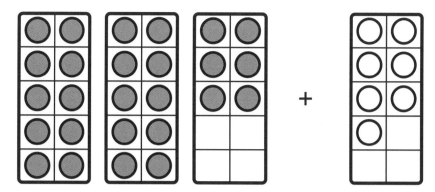

Show the addition as two jumps on a number line.

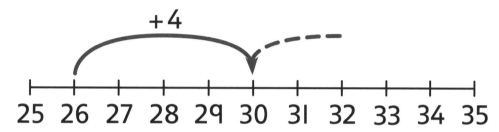

4 Complete the number sentences. Use the number lines to help you.

a) 18 + 5 = ☐

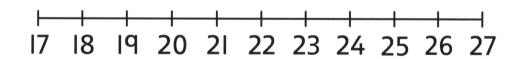

b) 43 + 8 = ☐

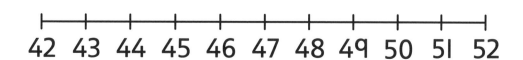

5 Complete each number sentence.

a) $84 + 7 = 84 + 6 + \boxed{} = \boxed{}$

b) $8 + 46 = 46 + \boxed{} + \boxed{} = \boxed{}$

6 Mary is working out 35 + 8.

Here is her working.

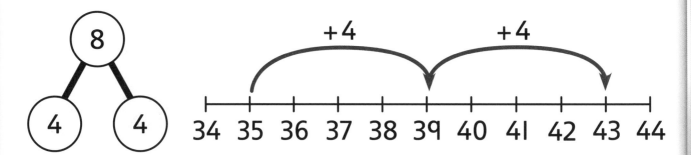

$35 + 8 = 35 + 4 + 4 = 43$

Tell a partner how Mary can improve her method.

Reflect

| 54 + 8 |

Discuss why you would add on 6 first and then 2.

Subtract across a 10

1 There are 13 butterflies.

5 fly away.

How many are left?

13 – 3 – 2 = ☐

So, 13 – 5 = ☐

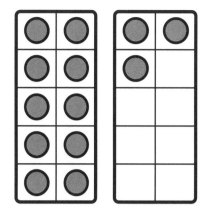

2 **a)** Work out 12 – 6 = ☐ .

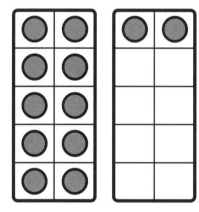

12 – ☐ – ☐ = ☐

b) Work out 12 – 8.

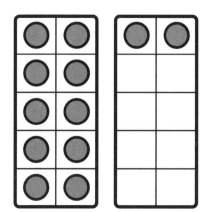

12 – ☐ – ☐ = ☐

3 **a)** Work out 15 − 9.

$\boxed{} - \boxed{} - \boxed{} = \boxed{}$

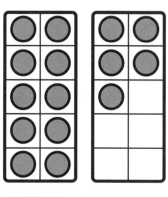

b) Work out 11 − 6 = $\boxed{}$.

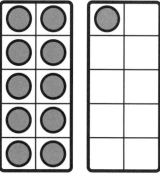

4 Work out 14 − 6.

5	6	7	8	9	10	11	12	13	14	15

14 − $\boxed{}$ − $\boxed{}$ = $\boxed{}$

5 Work out 15 − 7.

6	7	8	9	10	11	12	13	14	15	16

15 − $\boxed{}$ − $\boxed{}$ = $\boxed{}$

6 Complete the number sentences.

a) $14 - 9 = \boxed{}$

b) $15 - 9 = \boxed{}$

c) $12 - 8 = \boxed{}$

d) $14 - \boxed{} = 6$

e) $\boxed{} - 8 = 9$

Reflect

Show two ways you can work out $13 - 6$.

Date: _____

Subtract from a 10

Textbook 2A p124

1 Complete the number sentences.

a)

$10 - 5 =$ ▢

b)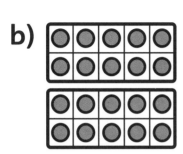

$20 - 5 =$ ▢

c)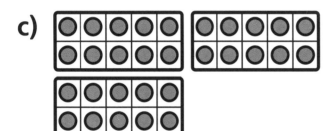

$30 - 5 =$ ▢

2 Complete the number sentences.

a) $10 - 1 =$ ▢

b) $10 - 2 =$ ▢

c) $10 - 3 =$ ▢

d) $10 - 4 =$ ▢

e) $50 - 1 =$ ▢

f) $30 - 3 =$ ▢

g) $90 - 4 =$ ▢

h) $70 - 1 =$ ▢

i) $40 - 2 =$ ▢

j) $80 - 3 =$ ▢

3 Find the missing numbers.

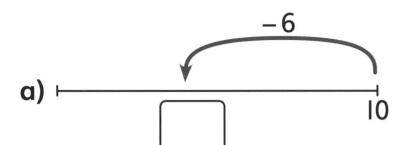

a)

$10 - 6 = \boxed{}$

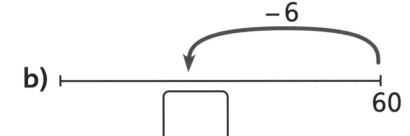

b)

$60 - 6 = \boxed{}$

4 Complete the number sentences.

a) $40 - \boxed{} = 32$

c) $100 - \boxed{} = 96$

b) $40 - \boxed{} = 38$

d) $100 - \boxed{} = 91$

5 Complete the number sentences.

a) $\boxed{} - 7 = 23$

e) $\boxed{} - 9 = 21$

b) $\boxed{} - 7 = 33$

f) $\boxed{} - 9 = 41$

c) $\boxed{} - 7 = 53$

g) $\boxed{} - 9 = 61$

d) $\boxed{} - 7 = 83$

h) $\boxed{} - 9 = 81$

6 Draw a line to join each matching pair.

CHALLENGE

| 50 + 7 | 50 + 4 | 50 + 3 | 60 + 4 | 60 + 6 | 60 + 2 |

| 70 – 6 | 70 – 8 | 70 – 4 | 60 – 3 | 60 – 7 | 60 – 6 |

Reflect

Work out the subtractions to complete the grid.

Talk about any patterns you notice with a partner.

10 – 0	10 – 2	10 – 4	10 – 6	10 – 8	10 – 10
20 – 0	20 – 2	20 – 4	20 – 6	20 – 8	20 – 10
40 – 0	40 – 2	40 – 4	40 – 6	40 – 8	40 – 10
60 – 0	60 – 2	60 – 4	60 – 6	60 – 8	60 – 10
80 – 0	80 – 2	80 – 4	80 – 6	80 – 8	80 – 10
100 – 0	100 – 2	100 – 4	100 – 6	100 – 8	100 – 10

Subtract a 1-digit number from a 2-digit number – across 10

1 Work out 42 – 6.

42 – ⬜ – ⬜ = ⬜

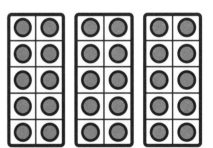

2 Work out 33 – 5.

33 – ⬜ – ⬜ = ⬜

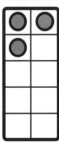

3 Work out 24 – 8.

24 – ⬜ – ⬜ = ⬜

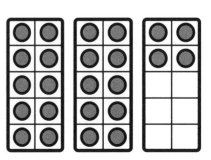

4 Complete each number sentence.

a) 36 – 9 = 36 – ☐ – ☐ = ☐

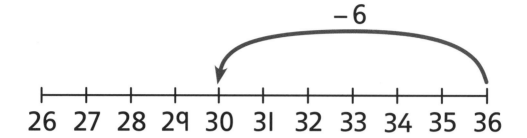

b) 63 – 9 = ☐ – ☐ – ☐ = ☐

c) 71 – 6 = ☐ – ☐ = ☐

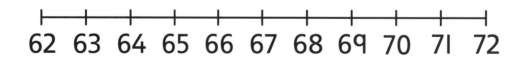

5 **a)** 65 – 8 = ☐

b) 43 – 8 = ☐

6 Work out the answers.

52 – 5 = ☐

62 – 5 = ☐

72 – 5 = ☐

Discuss what you notice with a partner.

Reflect

Hanna is working out 27 – 9. Here is her method.

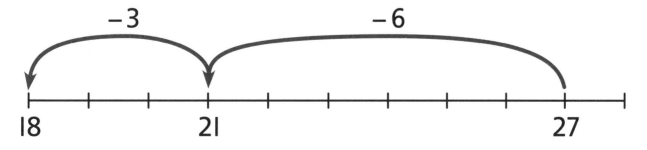

Discuss with a partner how to improve the method.

97

Date: _____

End of unit check

My journal

→ Textbook 2A p132

What methods would you use to work out the following?

36 + 2

36 + 9

36 – 2

36 – 9

_____

_____

_____

_____

These words will help you.

tens   ones

add   total

subtract

Power check

How do you feel about your work in this unit?

Power puzzle

Can you work out the value of each symbol?

63 + ★ = 68

★ + ◆ = 100

22 + 50 = ■

■ − ★ = ▲

★ = ☐

◆ = ☐

■ = ☐

▲ = ☐

Put the shapes in order. Start with the shape that has the smallest value.

Date: _____

10 more, 10 less

1 Complete the number sentences.

a)

10 more than 24 is ☐.

b)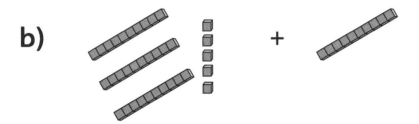

10 more than 35 is ☐.

2 Max has 53 cups.

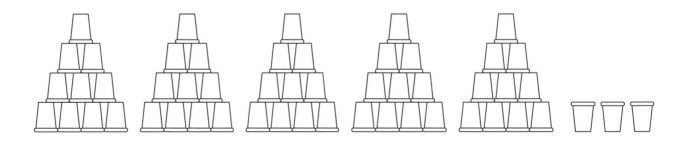

He gets 10 more.

How many cups does he have now?

Max has ☐ in total.

3 Complete the number tracks.

a)

| 44 | 54 | 64 | | | 94 |

b)

| 7 | 17 | 27 | | | | | 77 |

c)

| 78 | 68 | 58 | | | | 18 |

4 Complete the table.

10 less	Number	10 more
	30	
	72	
23		
		54

5 Complete each number sentence.

a) 10 more than 25 is ☐.

b) ☐ is 10 more than 73.

c) 10 less than 89 is ☐.

6 Complete the sentences.

CHALLENGE

One less than my number is 37.

10 more than Hassan's number is ☐.

10 less than Hassan's number is ☐.

Reflect

Choose a number from the number track.

48	49	50	51	52	53

Ask a partner to say 10 more than the number. Are they correct?

Now ask your partner to choose a number.

Say 10 less than this number. Are you correct?

Add and subtract 10s

1 Complete the number sentences.

a) 28 + 30 = ⬚

T	O

b) 42 + 20 = ⬚

T	O

I used number bonds to help me.

2 Complete the number sentences.

a) 51 + 30 = ⬚

b) 32 + 20 = ⬚

c) 22 + 40 = ⬚

d) 35 + 20 = ⬚

3 Complete the number sentences.

a) 53 − 20 = ☐

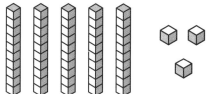

b) 94 − 50 = ☐

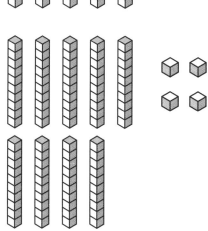

c) 76 − 30 = ☐

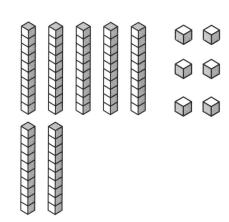

4 Complete the part-whole model and the bar model.

a)

84	
	50

5 Fill in the missing digits.

a) 82 – ▢0 = 52

b) 23 + ▢▢ = 63

6 Complete these number walls.

CHALLENGE

a)

50	18
38	

b)

74	
4	
20	

Reflect

Fill in the missing digits to complete the number sentences.

▢6 – ▢0 = 76   ▢6 – ▢0 = 36

Did you get the same as your partner?

Date: _____

Add two 2-digit numbers – add 10s and add 1s

1

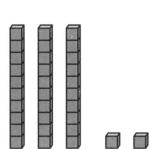 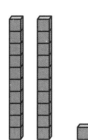

a) How many 10s in total? ☐ 10s

b) How many 1s in total? ☐ 1s

c) Work out 32 + 24 = ☐

2 Complete the number sentence.

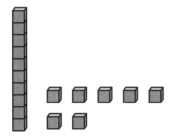 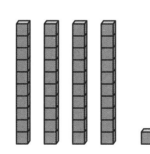

17 + 42 = ☐

3 Complete the number sentence.

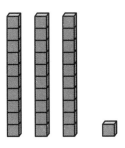 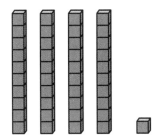 

31 + 45 = ☐

4 Complete the number sentences.

a) 25 + 23 = ☐

b) 53 + 12 = ☐

c) 72 + 11 = ☐

d) 43 + 43 = ☐

I'm going to use base 10 equipment to make each number. That will help me.

5

a) Add the 10s. There are ☐ tens.

b) Add the 1s. There are ☐ ones.

c) 28 + 14 = ☐

6 Use equipment to work out:

a) 35 + 27 = ☐

b) 28 + 36 = ☐

c) 49 + 17 = ☐

Reflect

Show or tell a partner how to add 32 and 42.

Add two 2-digit numbers – add more 10s then more 1s

1 Work out the additions.

Fill in the missing numbers on the number lines to help you.

a) 34 + 25 = ☐

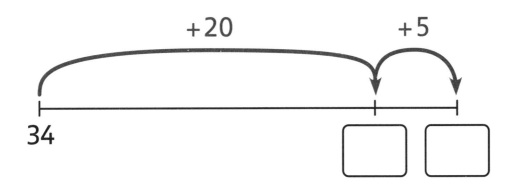

+20   +5

34

b) 42 + 34 = ☐

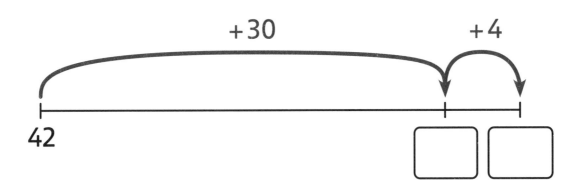

+30   +4

42

2 Complete the additions.

Fill in the jumps on the number lines to help you.

a) 45 + 13 = ☐

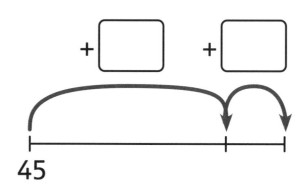

b) 52 + 16 = ☐

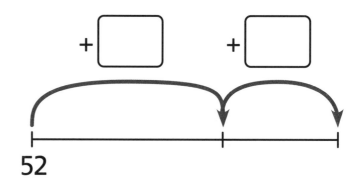

c) 16 + 52 = ☐

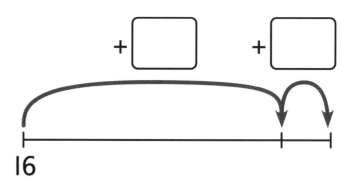

What is the same and what is different about part b) and part c)? Discuss with a partner.

3 Work out

48 + 15 = ☐

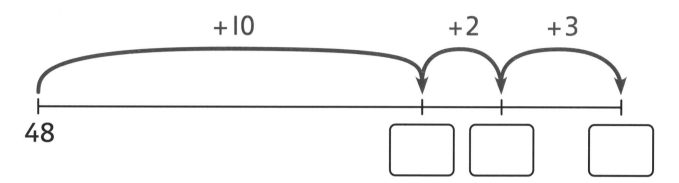

+10   +2   +3

48

☐ ☐   ☐

4 Solve these additions.

a) 26 + 18 = ☐

b) 35 + 27 = ☐

I can solve
some in
my head.

c) 45 + 5 = ☐

d) 18 + 28 = ☐

Reflect

Explain to your partner how you could add 17 and 67.

Date: _____

Subtract a 2-digit number from a 2-digit number – not across 10

1 Work out the subtractions.

Fill in the number line to help you.

a) 38 – 12 = ☐

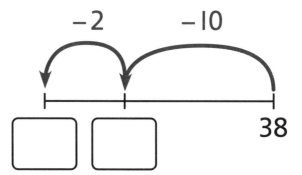

b) 45 – 32 = ☐

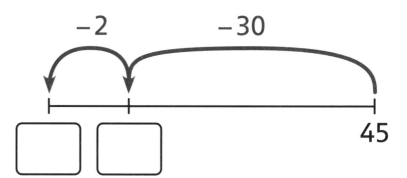

c) 78 – 24 = ☐

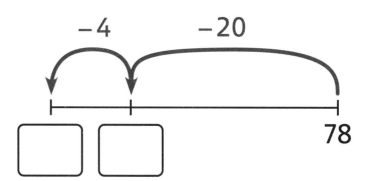

2 Work out

a) 67 − 25 = ☐

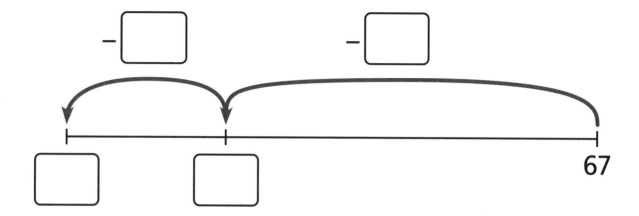

b) 78 − 25 = ☐

☐

c) 58 − 32 = ☐

☐

3 Kara and Chen are working out 48 – 36.

Show that they get the same answer.

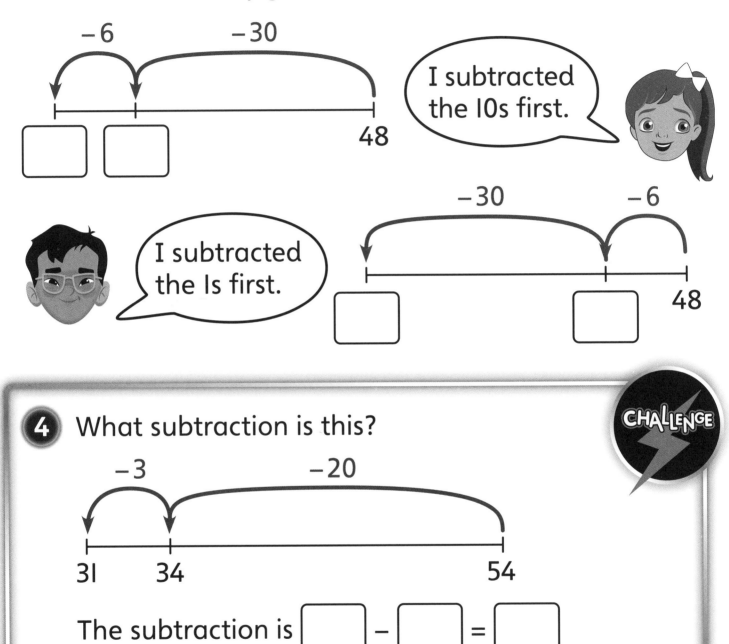

− 6   − 30

48

I subtracted the 10s first.

I subtracted the 1s first.

− 30   − 6

48

CHALLENGE

4 What subtraction is this?

− 3   − 20

31   34   54

The subtraction is ☐ − ☐ = ☐

Reflect

Discuss with a partner how to work out 74 – 23.

Subtract a 2-digit number from a 2-digit number – across 10

1 Complete the number sentences.

Fill in the number line to help you.

a) 52 − 25 = ☐

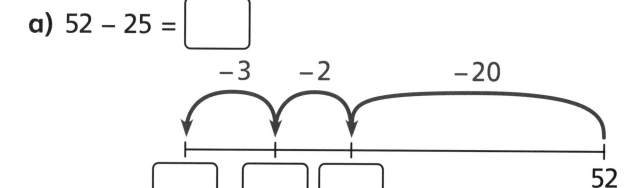

b) 41 − 16 = ☐

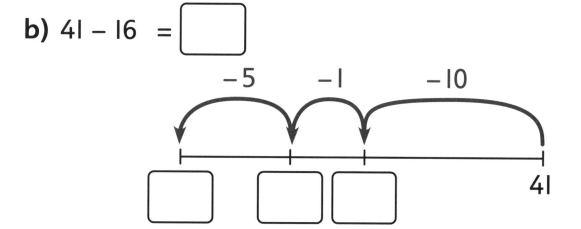

c) 74 − 26 = ☐

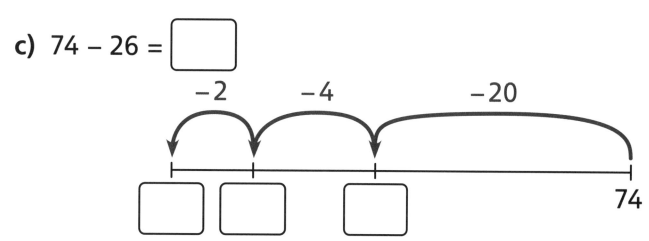

2 Complete the number sentences.

Fill in the number line to help you.

a) 63 – 18 = ⬜

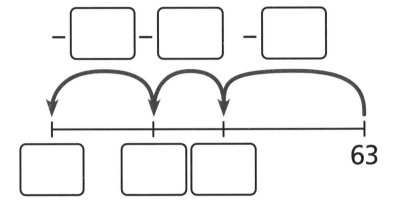

b) 63 – 28 = ⬜

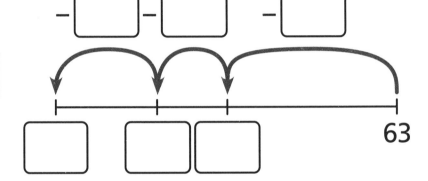

3 **a)** Work out 45 – 28 = ⬜

b) Work out 71 – 15 = ⬜

4 Here are six digit cards.

| 1 | 2 | 3 | 4 | 6 | 8 |

a) Use each card once to complete the subtraction.

☐☐ – ☐☐ = ☐☐

b) Find another way.

☐☐ – ☐☐ = ☐☐

Reflect

Discuss with a partner how you work out each of these.

| 43 + 15 | 45 + 18 | 45 – 12 | 45 – 17 |

Date: _____

How many more? How many fewer?

1 a) Find the difference between 7 and 3.

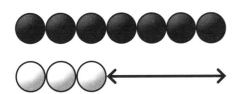

7 is ⬚ more than 3.

b) Find the difference between 8 and 6.

6 is ⬚ less than 8.

2 Find the missing numbers.

a)

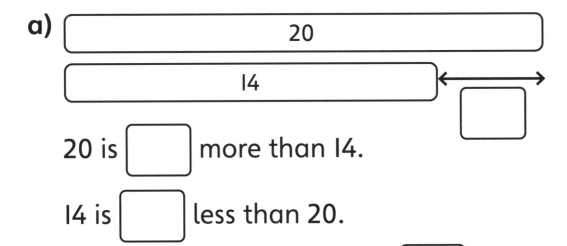

20 is ⬚ more than 14.

14 is ⬚ less than 20.

b)

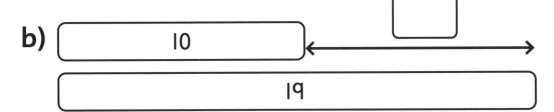

19 is ⬚ more than 10.

10 is ⬚ less than 19.

Textbook 2A p160

3 **a)** What is the difference between 35 and 25?

b) What is the difference between 10 and 100?

4 Pick a card to complete each sentence.

8   0   3   9

a) 7 is 2 less than ☐.

b) ☐ is 5 more than 3.

c) The difference between 9 and 6 is ☐.

d) 8 is ☐ more than 8.

5 Fill in the jumps on the number lines.

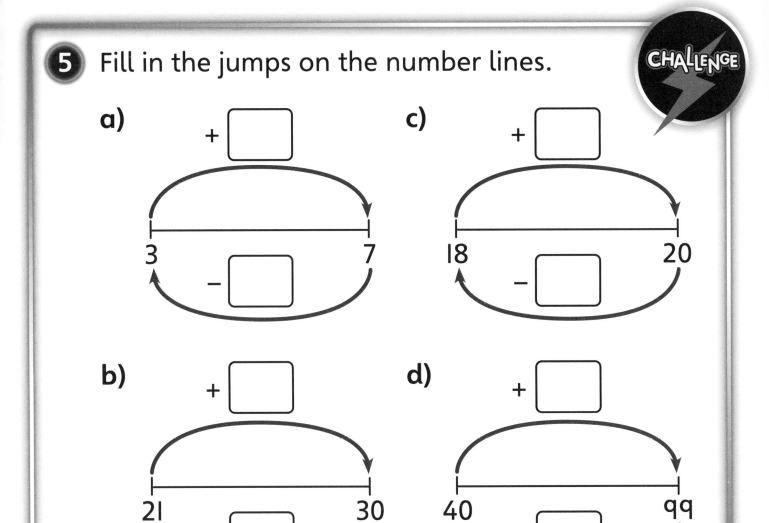

a)
+ ☐
3   7
− ☐

c)
+ ☐
18   20
− ☐

b)
+ ☐
21   30
− ☐

d)
+ ☐
40   99
− ☐

CHALLENGE

Reflect

Write down pairs of numbers with a difference of 10.

Subtraction – find the difference

→ Textbook 2A p164

1 **a)** Find the difference between 24 and 20.

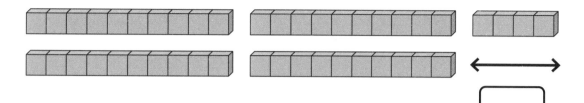

b) Complete the subtraction.

$$24 - 20 = \boxed{}$$

2 Complete the subtractions.

a)

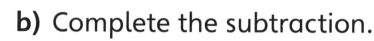

$$10 - 4 = \boxed{}$$

b)

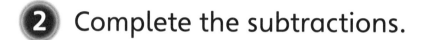

$$12 - 2 = \boxed{}$$

c)

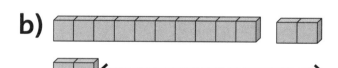

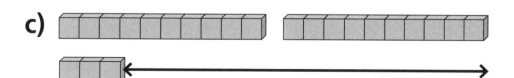

$$20 - 3 = \boxed{}$$

121

3 Find the difference between the two numbers.

a)

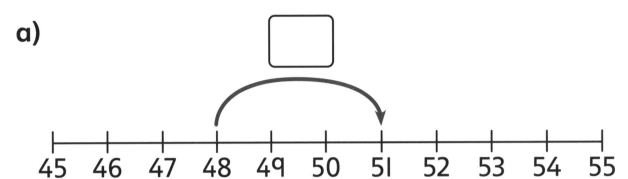

b)

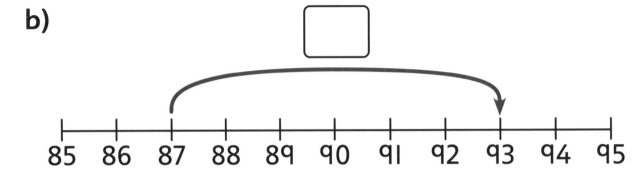

c)

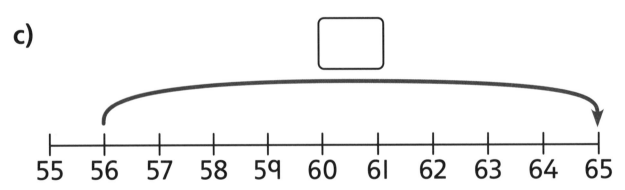

d) Complete the number sentences.

51 – 48 = ☐

93 – 87 = ☐

65 – 56 = ☐

4 Mo has 32 points. Kim has 29 points.

How many more points does Mo have?

5 Write down two pairs of numbers with a difference of 10.

☐ and ☐   ☐ and ☐

Now complete the subtractions.

☐ – ☐ = 10   ☐ – ☐ = 10

Reflect

Say a number. ☐

Ask a partner to say another number. ☐

What is the difference? ☐

Date: _____

Compare number sentences

1 Complete each number sentence.

a)

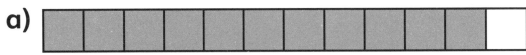

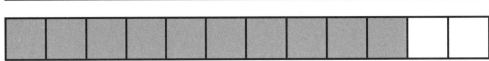

$11 + 1 = 10 + \boxed{}$

b)

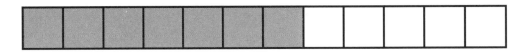

$6 + 6 = 7 + \boxed{}$

c)

$6 + 7 = 7 + \boxed{}$

d)

$10 + 6 = 8 + \boxed{}$

2 Add <, > or = to complete the number sentences.

a)

4 + 5 ◯ 4 + 6

b)

6 + 3 ◯ 5 + 4

c)

7 – 2 ◯ 7 – 4

3 Use <, > or = to make each number sentence correct.

a) 8 + 8 ◯ 7 + 7   **c)** 9 – 5 ◯ 9 – 8

b) 16 + 3 ◯ 16 – 1   **d)** 10 + 2 ◯ 9 + 3

Are there any I could do without working out the answers on both sides?

4 Find numbers that make these number sentences correct.

a) $3 + 7 > 3 + \boxed{}$

c) $5 + 14 > \boxed{} + 14$

b) $6 - 2 < 6 - \boxed{}$

d) $12 + \boxed{} = 6 + 12$

5 Find **one** number that makes **both** of these number sentences correct.

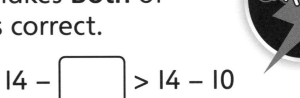

CHALLENGE

$7 + 6 < 6 + \boxed{}$ $14 - \boxed{} > 14 - 10$

Reflect

Make number sentences using the numbers **2, 3, 4** and **5**.

$\boxed{} + \boxed{} \bigcirc \boxed{} + \boxed{}$

$\boxed{} + \boxed{} \bigcirc \boxed{} + \boxed{}$

Ask a partner to check your number sentences.

Missing number problems

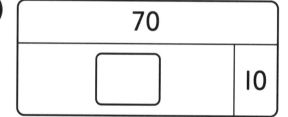

1 Find the missing parts and complete the number sentences.

a)

9	
5	☐

$5 + \boxed{} = 9$

d)

50	
☐	20

$\boxed{} + 20 = 50$

b)

10	
6	☐

$6 + \boxed{} = 10$

e)

70	
☐	10

$\boxed{} + 10 = 70$

c)

20	
2	☐

$2 + \boxed{} = 20$

f)

90	
60	☐

$60 + \boxed{} = 90$

2 Complete the number sentences.

a)

25   30

25 + ☐ = 30

c)

18   20

☐ + 18 = 20

b)

36   39

36 + ☐ = 39

d)

50   71

☐ + 50 = 71

3 Complete the number sentences.

a) 10 − ☐ = 5

d) 30 − ☐ = 10

b) 8 − ☐ = 6

e) 70 − ☐ = 40

c) 20 − ☐ = 17

f) 100 − ☐ = 20

4 Complete the number sentences.

a) $25 - \boxed{} = 20$

b) $89 - \boxed{} = 82$

5 Find the missing numbers.

a) $\boxed{} - 5 = 30$

b) $\boxed{} - 5 = 75$

What do you notice? Talk to a partner.

6 Solve the mystery!

CHALLENGE

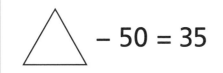 $- 50 = 35$

$50 - $ $= 17$

What is △ − ♡ ? $\boxed{}$

Reflect

Discuss with a partner what is missing: a whole or a part.

$\boxed{} - 3 = 27$

$\boxed{} + 19 = 40$

$28 - \boxed{} = 24$

Date: _____

Mixed addition and subtraction

1 Find the missing numbers.

a)
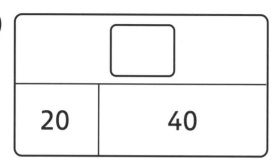

c)
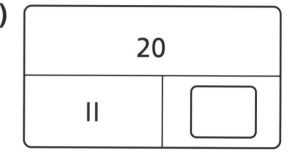

b)
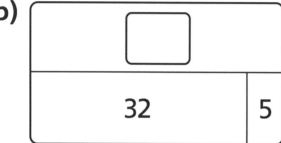

d)

2 Jan sells 31 cards on Monday.

She sells 57 cards on Tuesday.

How many does she sell in total?

?	
31	57

I will use the bar model to help me.

Jan sells ☐ cards in total.

3 72 people are watching a film.

26 of them are adults.

How many children are there?

	72	
26		?

There are ☐ children.

4 Eva rolls three dice.

Her total score is 13.

What is the missing number?

13		

The missing number is ☐.

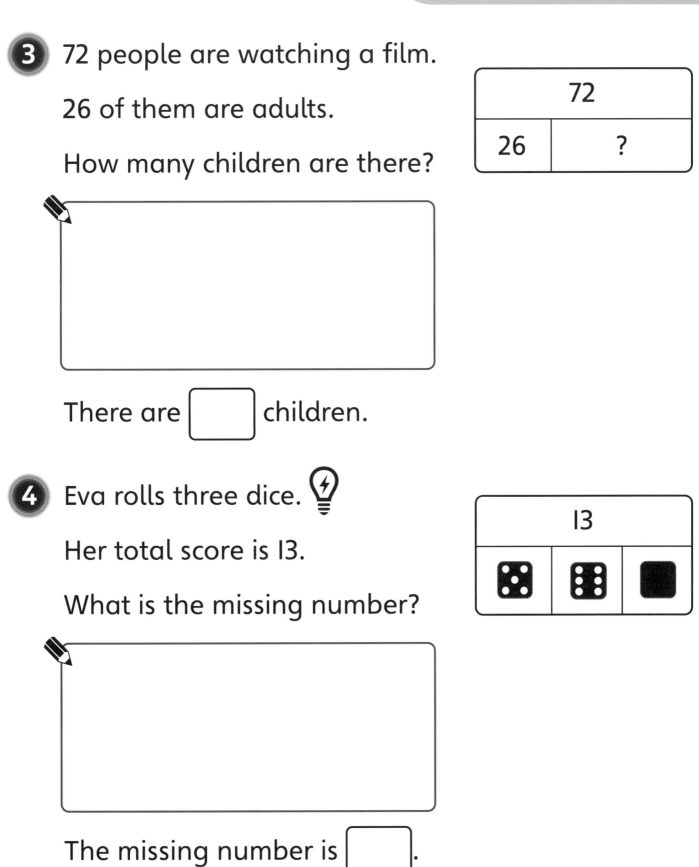

5 Two numbers total 72.

One of the numbers is 43.

What is the other number?

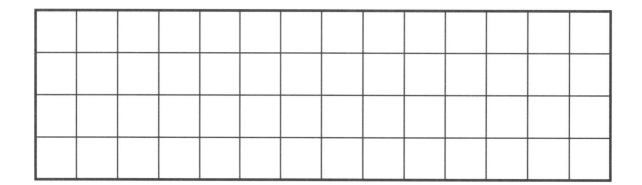

Reflect

Write a question to fit the bar model.

25	
17	?

Two-step problems

1 Katie has 35 flowers. Her mum has 12 fewer.

How many flowers does Katie's mum have?

Katie | 35 |

Mum | | ← 12 →

Katie's mum has ☐ flowers.

2 Abel has 6 cars. Jak has 9 cars. Kaya has 7 cars.

How many cars are there altogether?

There are ☐ cars altogether.

3 Sam scored 75 goals.

Jan scored 48 goals.

How many more goals did Sam score than Jan?

Sam scored ☐ goals more than Jan.

4 Megan is 25 years old.

Kris is 16 years older than Megan.

What is the total of their ages?

The total of their ages is ☐.

5 Two buses have 72 people on them, in total.

The first has 28 people on it.

How many more people are on the second bus than on the first?

CHALLENGE

First bus

Second bus

?

72

There are ☐ more people on the second bus than on the first.

Reflect

Tell a partner which question you found easiest.

Date: _____

End of unit check

My journal

Circle the odd one out.

Prove it.

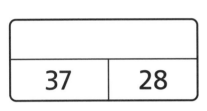

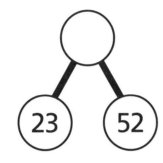

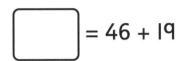

$\boxed{}$ = 46 + 19

It is the odd one out because _____

_____

_____ .

These words will help you.

ones   **tens**

add   subtract

equals

Power check

How do you feel about your work in this unit?

Power puzzle

Using the digit cards 1–9, make three unequal piles that total the same amount.

| 1 | 2 | 3 | 4 | 5 | 6 | 7 | 8 | 9 |

Pile 1: _____

Pile 2: _____

Pile 3: _____

Can you solve the puzzle with equal piles?

How many ways can you find?

Now try with the cards 2 to 10.

Date: _____

Recognise 2D and 3D shapes

1 **a)** Colour in all the triangles.

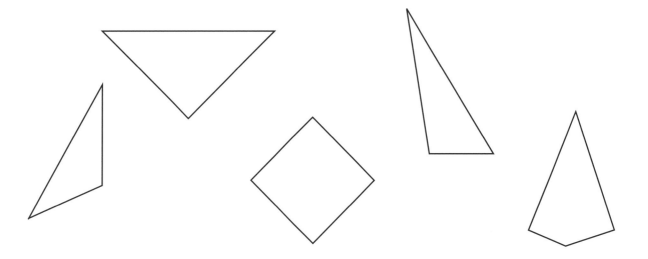

b) Colour in all the squares.

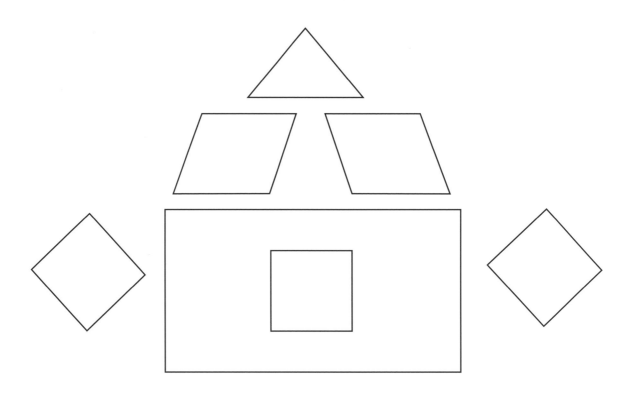

2 Here are some 3D shapes.

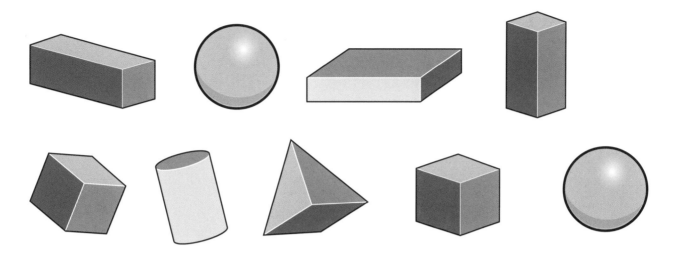

a) Circle the pyramid.

b) Colour the cubes.

c) Tick the spheres.

3 How many cuboids, pyramids and spheres are there in this picture?

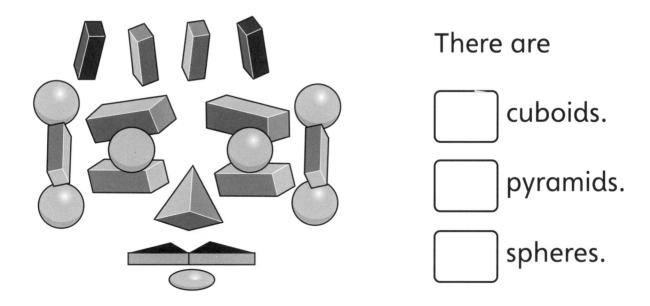

There are

cuboids.

pyramids.

spheres.

4 Sara and Mo are drawing around 3D shapes.

Write the name of the 2D shape each child will draw.

Sara will draw a

_____ .

Mo will draw a

_____ .

Reflect

Name three 2D shapes and three 3D shapes.

Point to them in the classroom or on the page.

Count sides on 2D shapes

1 Complete the table.

Shape	Name	Number of sides
△	tr_angle	
⬠	pent_g_n	
◇	squ_r_	
▭	r_ctangl_	4
⬡	hex_g_n	

2 Match the shape to the sentence.

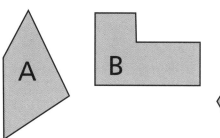 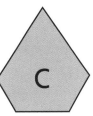  

Shape D has ☐ sides.

Shape A has ☐ sides.

Shape ____ has more than 6 sides.

Shape ____ has 5 sides.

Shape ____ has an even number of sides.

> There is one sentence for each shape.

3 Complete the shapes.

How many sides does each shape have?

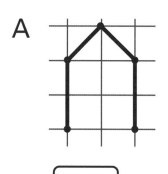   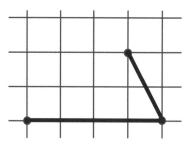   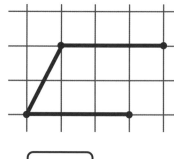

A ☐ sides   B ☐ sides   C ☐ sides

4 **a)** Rob makes 5 triangles using straws.

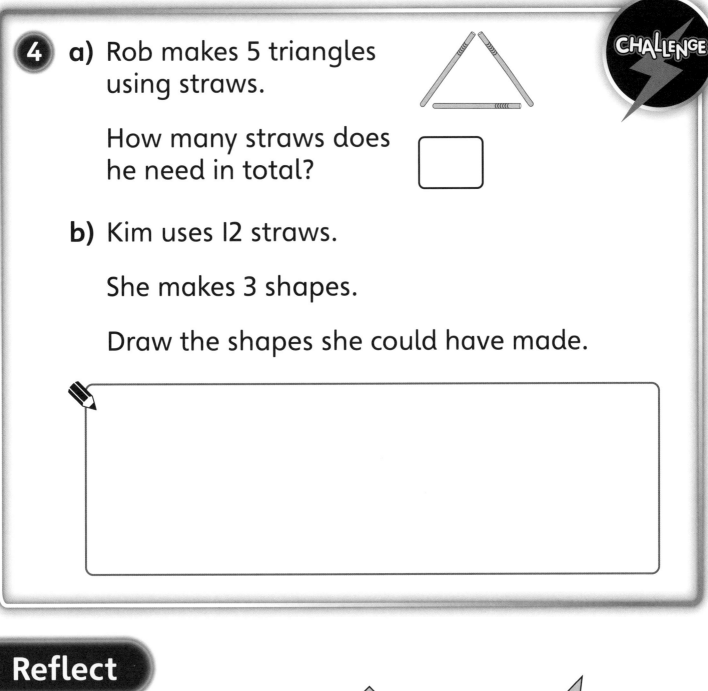

CHALLENGE

How many straws does he need in total?

b) Kim uses 12 straws.

She makes 3 shapes.

Draw the shapes she could have made.

Reflect

Which shape is the odd one out? Why?

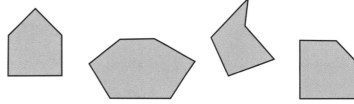

Date: _____

Count vertices on 2D shapes

1 Match the shapes to the number of vertices.

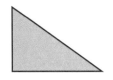  

[3 vertices] [4 vertices] [5 vertices]

2 Complete the table.

Shape	Number of vertices
parallelogram	
arrow quadrilateral	
pentagon (house)	
hexagon	

3 Complete the sentences with the words below.

| square | pentagon | triangle | rectangle |

A _____ has 5 vertices and 5 sides.

A shape with 4 vertices could be a _____

or a _____ .

A _____ has fewer vertices than a square.

4

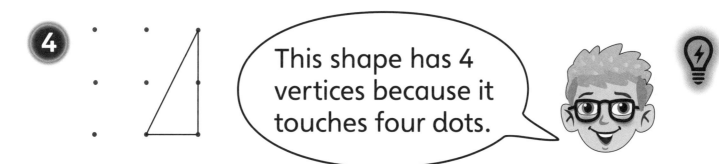

This shape has 4 vertices because it touches four dots.

Explain Toby's mistake to a partner.

5 Here is a hexagon.

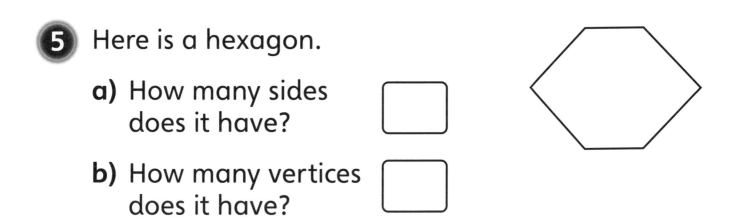

a) How many sides does it have? ☐

b) How many vertices does it have? ☐

6 **a)** Draw two different shapes with four vertices.

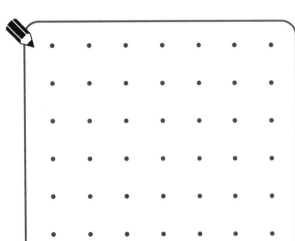

b) Draw two different shapes with five vertices.

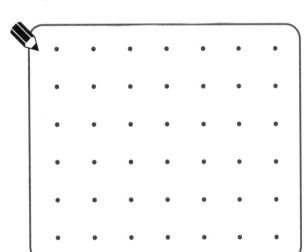

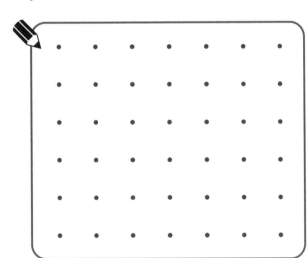

Reflect

Discuss with a partner what is the same and what is different.

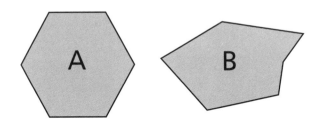

Date: _____

Draw 2D shapes

 These are the dots for the corners of polygons.

Complete each polygon.

One has been done for you.

Write the name of each shape.

Use a ruler to join the dots.

a)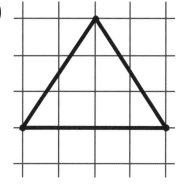

_____

c)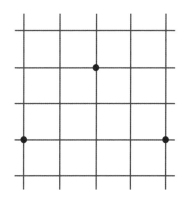

_____

e)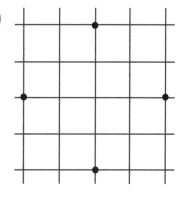

_____

b)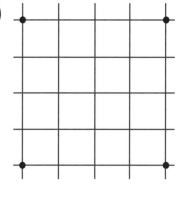

_____

d)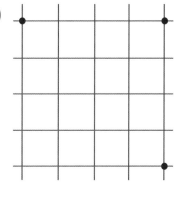

_____

f)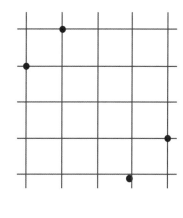

_____

2 Draw one more dot to make a rectangle.

a) 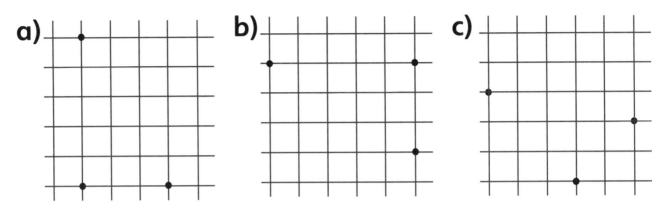 b) c)

3 Copy the triangles from the square grid to the plain paper.

One has been started for you.

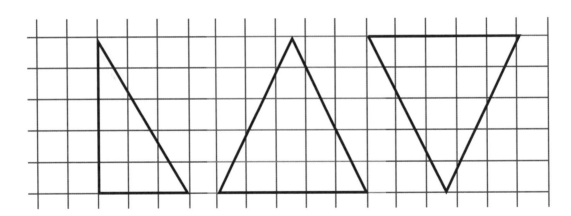

4 Draw as many different squares as you can on these grids.

CHALLENGE

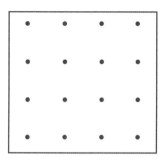 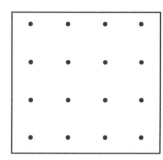 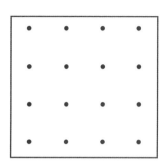

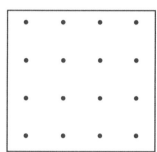 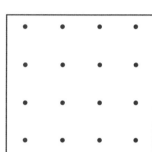 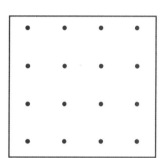

Reflect

Give three instructions for how to draw this shape accurately.

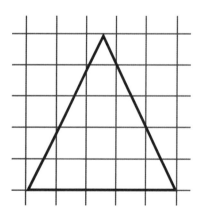

● First, _____.

● Then, _____.

● Finally, _____.

●

Date: _____

Lines of symmetry on shapes

1 Draw a line of symmetry on each of these shapes.

2 Complete the symmetrical shapes.

a)
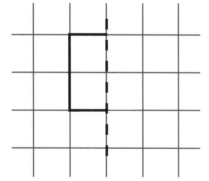

c)
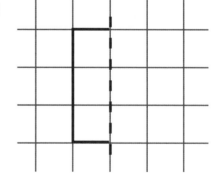

b)
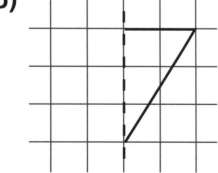

d)
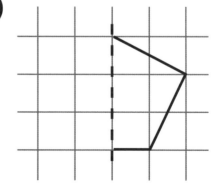

150

3 Match the folded shapes to the whole shapes.

4 Tick or cross each shape to show whether the line of symmetry is correct.

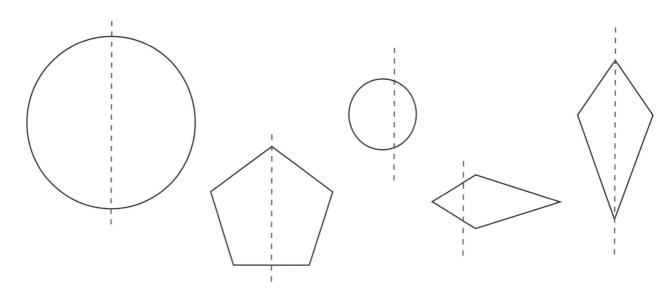

5 Make a symmetrical shape by folding and cutting a piece of paper.

Draw the shape here and show the line of symmetry.

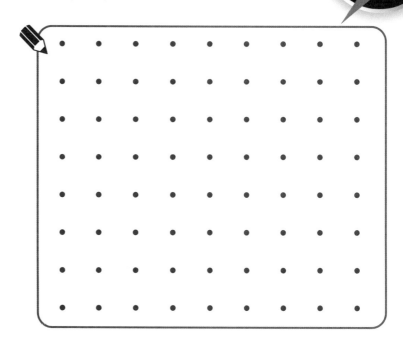

Reflect

I have a shape. It has fewer than 5 vertices. It is symmetrical.

Explain to a partner what this shape could look like.

Now draw the shape.

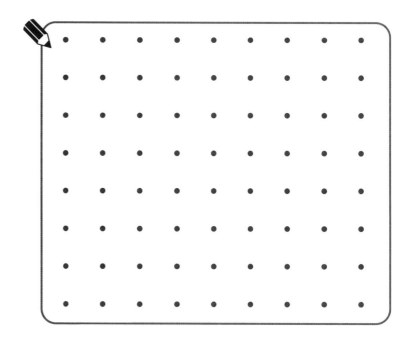

Sort 2D shapes

→ Textbook 2A p208

1 Draw lines to connect each shape to the correct group.

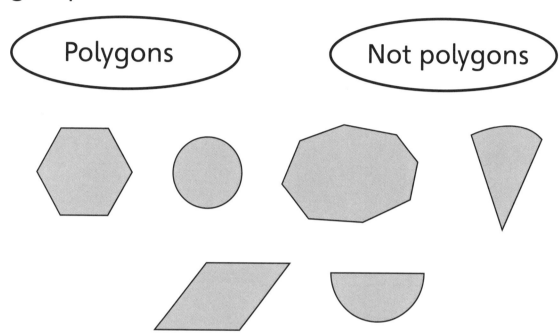

Polygons

Not polygons

2 Put the shapes in order.

Start from the shape with the fewest number of vertices.

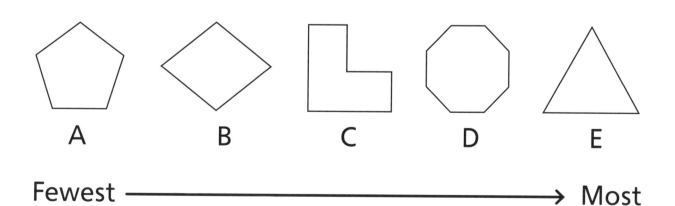

A   B   C   D   E

Fewest ─────────────────────→ Most

3 Match the label to the group.

| fewer than 5 vertices | curved sides | 5 vertices |

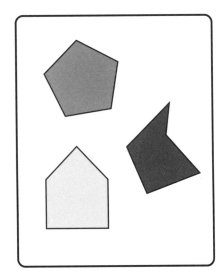
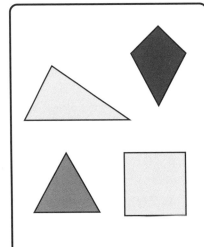
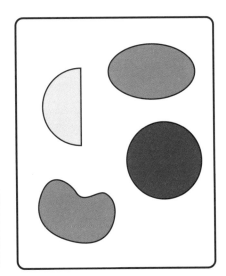

4 Draw two different shapes to go in each group.

| a shape with 3 vertices | a shape with 4 vertices |

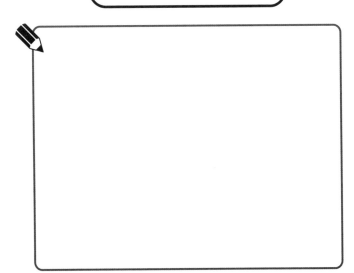

5 Draw a shape that can go into each group.

CHALLENGE

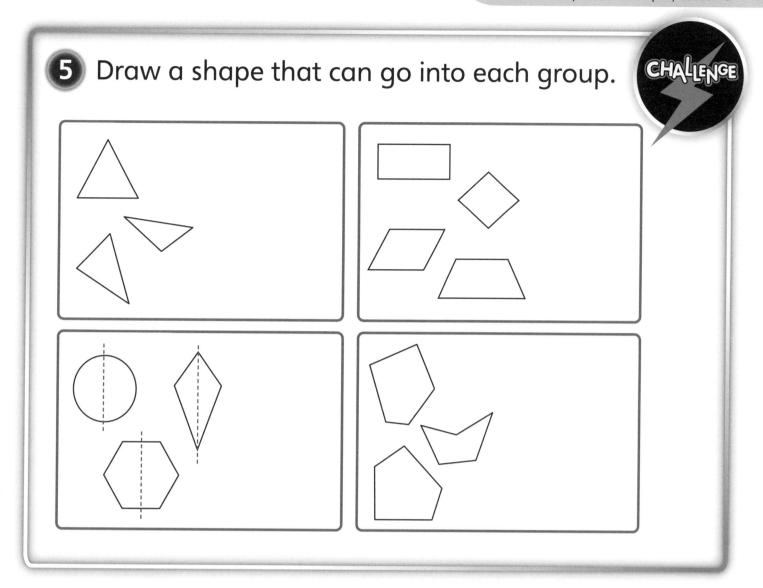

Reflect

Explain how to sort these shapes into two groups.

Each group should have the same number of shapes.

Date: _____

Make patterns with 2D shapes

1 Show the repeating part of each pattern.

The first one has been done for you.

a)

b)

c)

d)

2 Circle the shapes that complete the patterns.

a)

b)

3 Draw the next two shapes for each pattern.

a) 1   2   3   4   5   6   ...   7   8

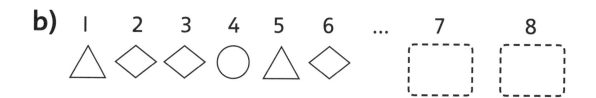

b) 1   2   3   4   5   6   ...   7   8

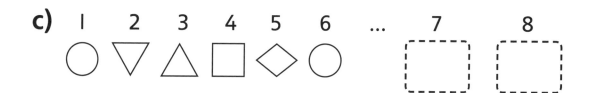

c) 1   2   3   4   5   6   ...   7   8

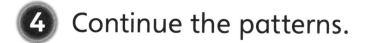

d) What shape would be in the
   20th position in pattern a)?

4 Continue the patterns.

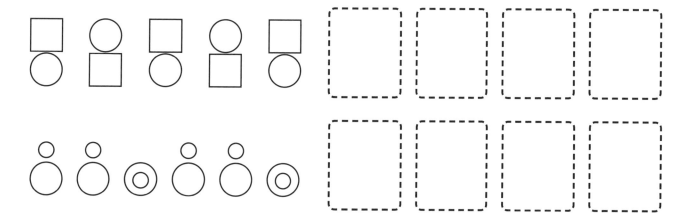

5 Complete these grids by following the patterns.

a)

○	●	◯	⬤
△	▲	△	▲
◇		◇	◆
	⬠	⬠	

b)

○	⬤	◯	●
⬠		⬟	⬠
◇	◆	◇	
▲	△		△

Reflect

Draw your own pattern.

Date: _____

Count faces on 3D shapes

→ Textbook 2A p216

1 Complete the table.

Shape	Name	Number of faces
	cu_e	
	pyr_m_d	
	cu_oi_	
	py_a_id	

2 Match each 3D shape to its faces.

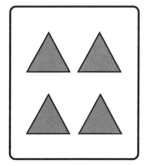 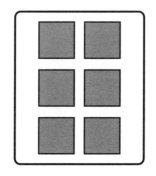 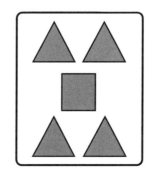 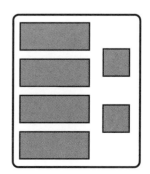

3 Complete each sentence.

hemisphere   sphere   cylinder   cone

A cylinder has 2 circle faces and ☐ curved surface.

A _____ has 0 faces and ☐ curved surface.

A _____ and a _____ both have I circle face and I curved surface.

4 Write the letters of the shapes each child could have.

A   B   C   D   E

I have 3 shapes. They are all the same. In total there are 12 faces.

I have 3 shapes that are different. In total there are 15 faces.

160

5 **a)**

 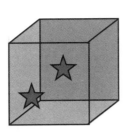

Ned puts 2 stickers on each face of this cube.

How many stickers does he need in total?

b)

Sophie puts a sticker on each face of her shape.

She uses 2 stickers in total.

Circle Sophie's shape.

Reflect

Name a 3D shape.

Challenge a partner to tell you the shape of its faces.

Then ask your partner to challenge you in the same way.

Date: _____

Count edges on 3D shapes

 How many edges does each shape have?

a) 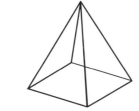  edges

b) 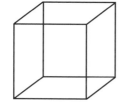  edges

c)   edges

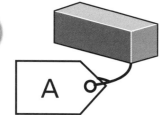 A 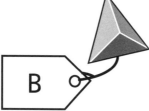 B 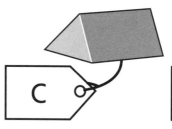 C  D

a) How many edges does shape A have? ☐

b) Which shape has fewer edges than shape A? ☐

c) Which shape has 4 fewer edges than A? ☐

3 Complete the sentences.

cube   triangular prism   square-based pyramid

A _____ has 6 faces and 12 edges.

A _____ has 5 faces and 9 edges.

A _____ has 5 faces and 8 edges.

4 Not all prisms have triangular ends.

Complete the sketch and write the number of edges for each.

A pentagonal prism has [   ] edges.

A hexagonal prism has [   ] edges.

This prism has [   ] edges.

This prism has [   ] edges.

5 **a)** Maddy made these shapes using sticks.

CHALLENGE

How many sticks did she use?

Maddy used ☐ sticks

Reflect

Discuss the difference between an edge and a face with a partner.

Count vertices on 3D shapes

→ Textbook 2A p224

1 Complete the table.

Shape	Number of vertices

I count vertices where edges meet.

2 Complete these sentences.

a) 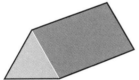 has ☐ vertices.

b)  has ☐ vertices.

c) 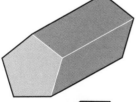 has ☐ vertices.

d) 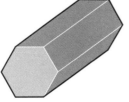 has ☐ vertices.

3 Match the shapes to the number of vertices.

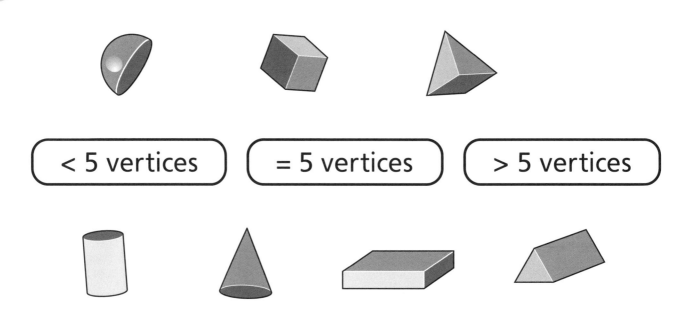

4 **a)** Circle the 2 shapes that have a total of 14 vertices.

b) Circle the 3 shapes that have a total of 17 vertices.

5 Complete the drawings for these pyramids.

Write the number of faces, edges and vertices for each one.

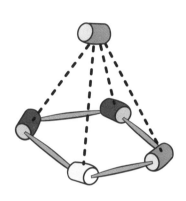

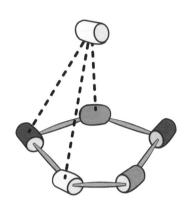

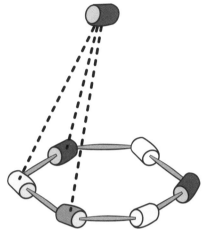

Faces = ☐   Faces = ☐   Faces = ☐

Edges = ☐   Edges = ☐   Edges = ☐

Vertices = ☐   Vertices = ☐   Vertices = ☐

Reflect

What is your favourite 3D shape? _____

How many vertices does it have? ☐

Compare with other people on your table.

Date: _____

Sort 3D shapes

1 Circle the shapes that do not belong in each group.

Has a curved surface	Has more than 1 square face	Has fewer than 6 vertices

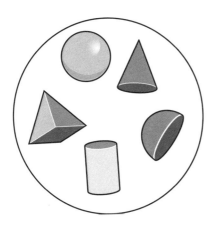 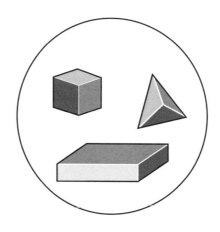 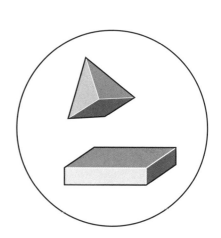

2 **a)** Circle the shapes with more than 3 faces.

b) Circle the shapes with fewer than 7 edges.

3 Tick the shape that could go in both groups.

Has a curved surface   Has no circular face

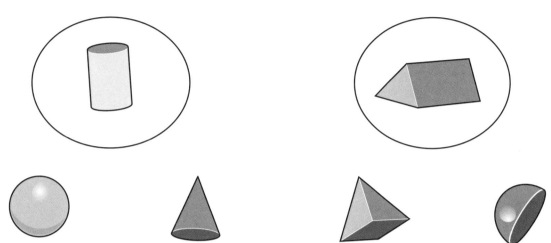

4 Choose headings to sort these shapes into 2 groups.

Make sure no shape is left out.

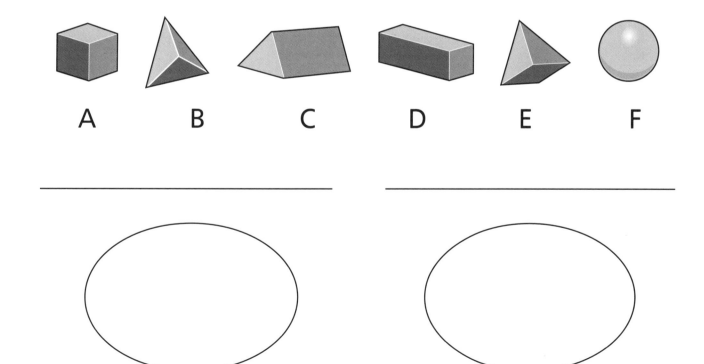

A   B   C   D   E   F

_____   _____

5

 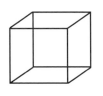 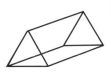

A　　　B　　　C　　　D　　　E

CHALLENGE

Put the shapes in order by the number of edges.

Fewest ————————————————→ Most

Now put the shapes in order by the number of vertices.

Fewest ————————————————→ Most

Reflect

Discuss with a partner 2 different ways to sort these 4 shapes into 2 different groups.

I will sort them so there are the same number of shapes in each group.

Make patterns with 3D shapes

1 These patterns are symmetrical.

Write the names of the missing shapes.

a)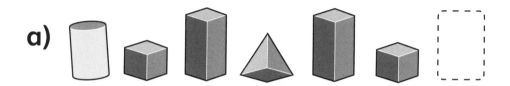

_____

b)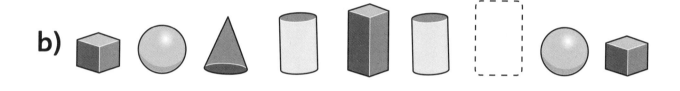

_____

2 Circle the next shape in the sequence.

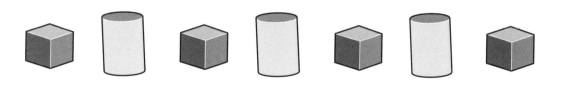

3 Draw your own pattern using these shapes.

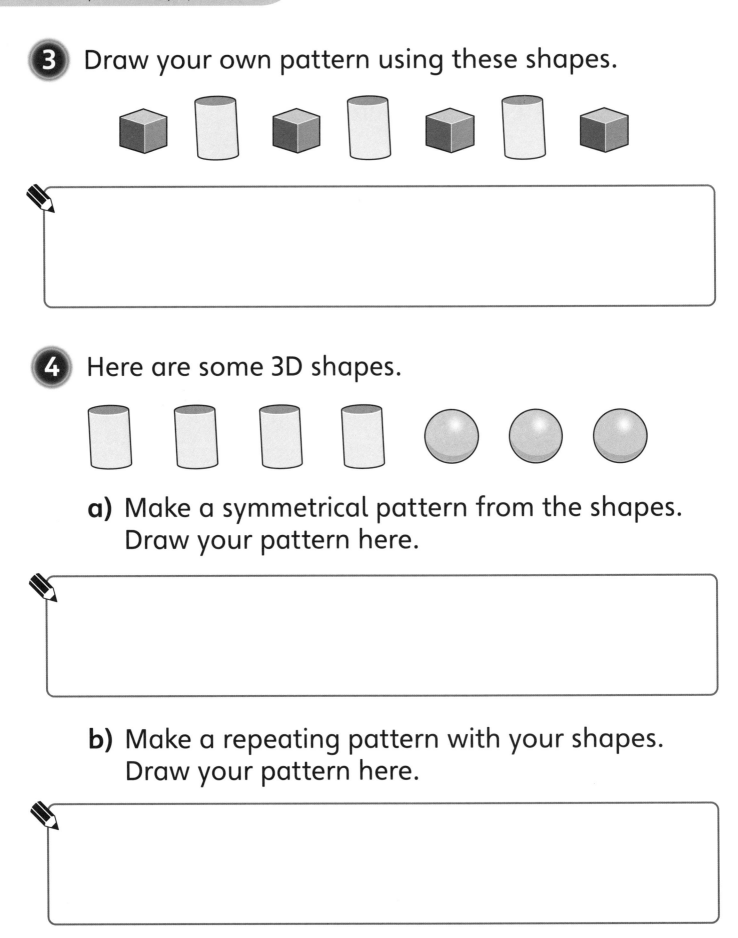

4 Here are some 3D shapes.

a) Make a symmetrical pattern from the shapes.
Draw your pattern here.

b) Make a repeating pattern with your shapes.
Draw your pattern here.

5 **a)** Nat made a symmetrical pattern using 3 shapes.

CHALLENGE

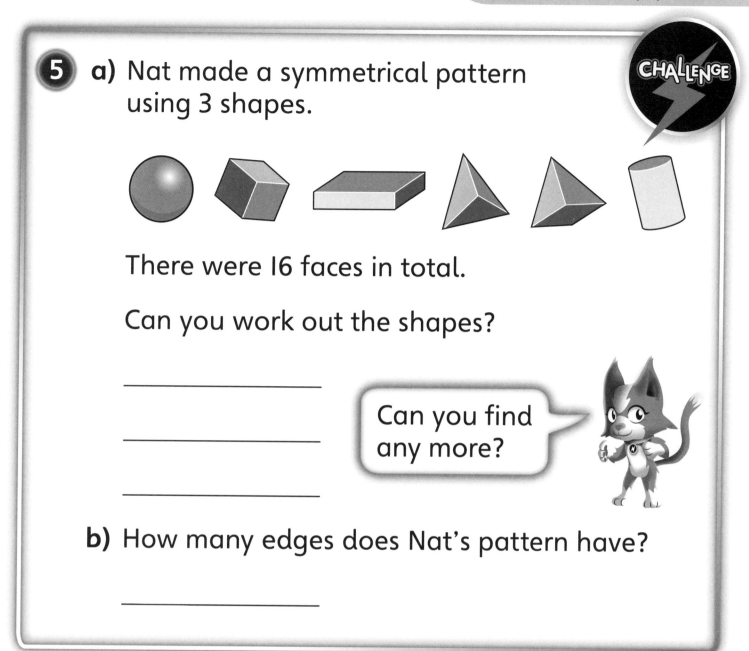

There were 16 faces in total.

Can you work out the shapes?

_____

_____

_____

Can you find any more?

b) How many edges does Nat's pattern have?

_____

Reflect

Explain to a partner the difference between a symmetrical pattern and a repeating pattern.

Date: _____

End of unit check

My journal

→ Textbook 2A p236

Theo has a square.

He draws 2 straight lines on it and then cuts along them.

Now he has 3 new shapes.

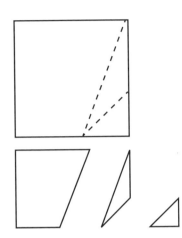

He counts the number of vertices for each new shape.

Find a way to cut the square into 3 shapes so each shape has a different number of vertices.

Is there more than one way?

Draw your shapes.

These words will help you.

vertices

hexagon   triangle

sides   pentagon

Power check

How do you feel about your work in this unit?

Power puzzle

Take 24 cubes.

How many different cuboids can you make by joining them together?

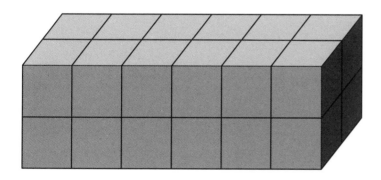

Take 27 cubes.

How many different cuboids can you make with them?

My Power Points

Colour in the ☆ to show what you have learnt.

Colour in the ☺ if you feel happy about what you have learnt.

Unit I
I can …

☆ ☺ Count numbers to 100
☆ ☺ Use different ways to show numbers to 100
☆ ☺ Use place value grids to make and compare numbers
☆ ☺ Compare and order numbers to 100
☆ ☺ Count in 2s, 5s and 10s
☆ ☺ Count in 3s

Unit 2
I can …

☆ ☺ Use related number facts
☆ ☺ Compare number sentences
☆ ☺ Make number bonds to 100
☆ ☺ Add and subtract 10s
☆ ☺ Add and subtract 1s
☆ ☺ Add a 2-digit and a 1-digit number
☆ ☺ Subtract a 1-digit number from a 2-digit number

Unit 3

I can …

☆ ☺ Add two 2-digit numbers

☆ ☺ Subtract 2-digit numbers

☆ ☺ Find the difference between two numbers

☆ ☺ Solve word problems using a bar model

Unit 4

I can …

☆ ☺ Recognise 2D and 3D shapes

☆ ☺ Count the sides and vertices on 2D shapes

☆ ☺ Learn about symmetry

☆ ☺ Count the faces, edges and vertices on 3D shapes

☆ ☺ Sort 2D and 3D shapes

Wow! Look how much we can do!

You can use these for your working out.

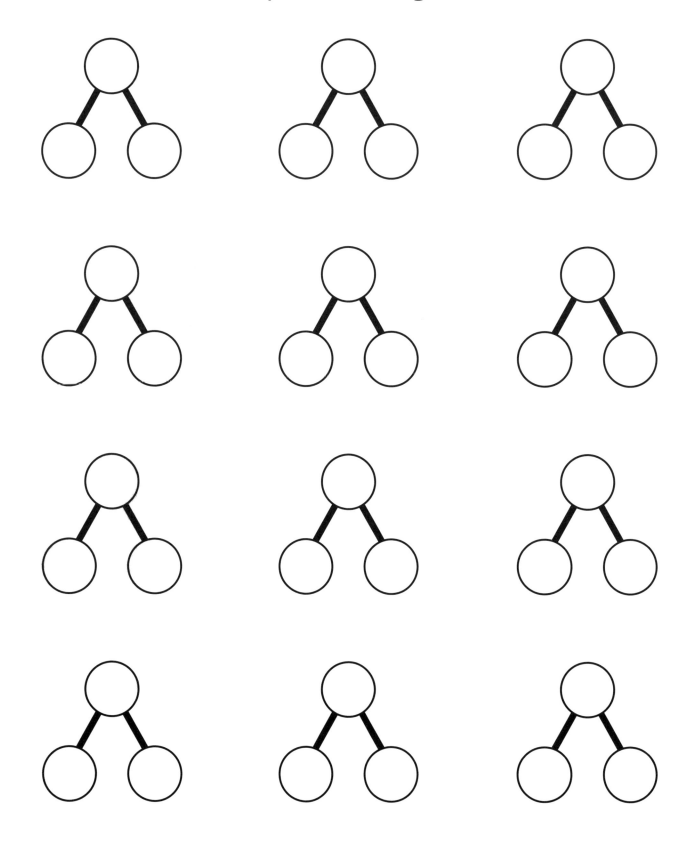

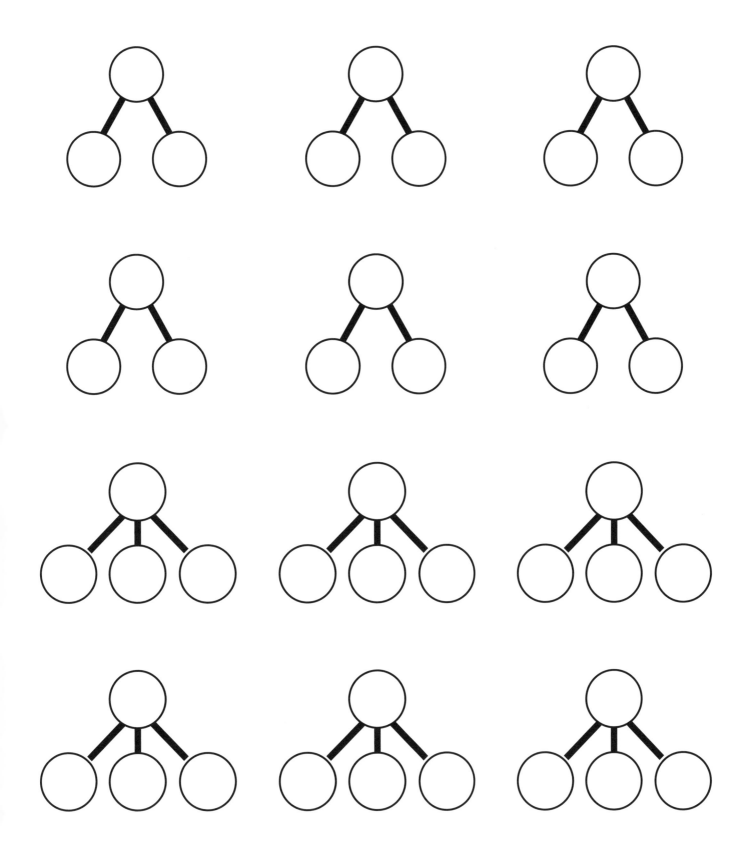

You can use these for your working out.

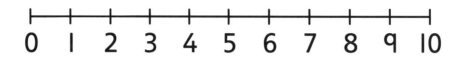

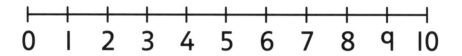

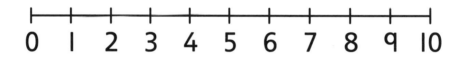

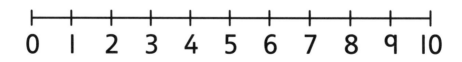

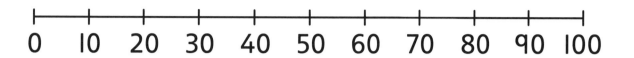

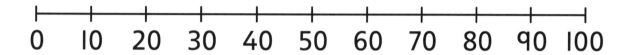

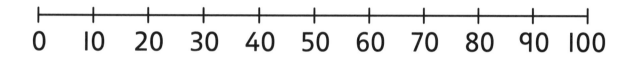

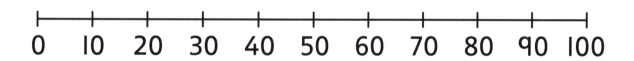

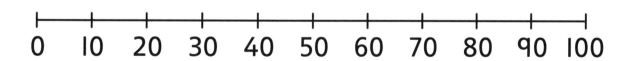

Published by Pearson Education Limited, 80 Strand, London, WC2R 0RL.

www.pearsonschools.co.uk

Text © Pearson Education Limited 2017, 2022
Edited by Pearson and Florence Production Ltd
First edition edited by Pearson and Haremi Ltd
Designed and typeset by Pearson and Florence Production Ltd
First edition designed and typeset by Kamae Design
Original illustrations © Pearson Education Limited 2017, 2022
Illustrated by Laura Arias, Fran and David Brylewski, Nigel Dobbyn, Adam Linley, Nadene Naude
and Dusan Pavlic at Beehive Illustration; and Florence Production Ltd and Kamae Design
Cover design by Pearson Education Ltd
Front and back cover illustrations by Will Overton at Advocate Art and Nadene Naude at
Beehive Illustration
Series editor: Tony Staneff; Lead author: Josh Lury
Authors (first edition): Tony Staneff, Josh Lury, Kelsey Brown, Liu Jian, Zhang Dan and
Wang Mingming
Consultant (first edition): Professor Liu Jian

The rights of Tony Staneff and Josh Lury to be identified as authors of this work have been
asserted by them in accordance with the Copyright, Designs and Patents Act 1988.

First published 2017
This edition first published 2022

26 25
10 9

British Library Cataloguing in Publication Data
A catalogue record for this book is available from the British Library

ISBN 978 1 292 41939 8

Printed in the UK by Bell & Bain Ltd, Glasgow

For Power Maths online resources, go to:
www.activelearnprimary.co.uk

Note from the publisher
Pearson has robust editorial processes, including answer and fact checks, to ensure the accuracy of
the content in this publication, and every effort is made to ensure this publication is free of errors.
We are, however, only human, and occasionally errors do occur. Pearson is not liable for any
misunderstandings that arise as a result of errors in this publication, but it is our priority to ensure
that the content is accurate. If you spot an error, please do contact us at resourcescorrections@
pearson.com so we can make sure it is corrected.